Ground Floor

Queen Victoria's favourite Prime Minister, Benjamin Disraeli, Earl of Beaconsfield, signed the Visitors' Book when he visited Hertford House in 1878. The Hall appears almost exactly as it did then.

Beaconsfield,
in this palace of genius
fancy & taste.
July 26 – 1878.

Edwin Landseer *The Arab Tent*
English 1866 (153.6 x 226.4cm)

Queen Victoria gave Landseer many commissions and knighted him in 1850. *The Arab Tent* depicts a menagerie of contented animals. An Arab mare and foal lie on an oriental carpet. A monkey and a baboon, which clutches an orange and wears an earring, nestle amongst palm leaves on the roof of the tent. Persian hounds sleep on a soft bed of rugs and skins. Landseer, who specialised in animal subjects, sold *The Arab Tent* to the Prince of Wales (later Edward VII). Landseer was also extremely popular with ordinary Victorians who knew his paintings through exhibitions and engravings.

A Guide to the Wall

Grania Lyster

Ground Floor

First Floor

Lower Ground Floor

Emmanuel Hannaux *Sir Richard Wallace* French 1899 (66cm high)

Charles Auguste Lebourg *Lady Wallace* French 1872 (71cm high)

A It was 16 February 1897. In *The Times* newspaper one could read of railway construction in China and, in London, 'Weather: dull, 41° F.' On this unremarkable day, a French woman, Amélie-Julie-Charlotte, died in Hertford House at the age of 78 and Britain received its largest-ever private bequest. It was the year that Bram Stoker's *Dracula* was published and Queen Victoria celebrated her Diamond Jubilee.

Lady Wallace, c.1890

Amélie-Julie-Charlotte was the widow of Sir Richard Wallace. For seven years she had led a solitary existence in Hertford House with her elderly red-setter, her late husband's French-speaking secretary and a plentiful supply of long black cheroots. Lady Wallace had lived in England only since the age of 52 and had never really felt at home. Yet she left her staggering collection of art to the British nation. News of the bequest, with its whispers of vast riches, illegitimacy and scandal, was lapped up by a gossip-hungry public. But then the family's exploits had been entertaining the British public since 1807 when Sir Richard Wallace's great-grandmother began a 12-year liaison with the future George IV.

The Wallace Collection was opened to the public as a national museum on 22 June 1900. Its first visitors were delighted, amazed and bemused.

A The 2nd Marquess of Hertford bought the lease of Hertford House in 1797. The 2nd Marchioness was a great hostess and, in the first three decades of the 19th century, the house was a landmark for fashionable London society. When the dowager 2nd Marchioness died in 1834, her son, the 3rd Marquess, was living in Dorchester House on Park Lane. He let Hertford House to the French Government as its Embassy. When he died in 1842 the house was left to his son, the 4th Marquess, who was living in Paris and had no intention of moving back to London. The French Embassy's lease continued for another eight years and then the house was left uninhabited for twenty years. It was used as a storehouse for the 4th Marquess' rapidly increasing collection of art. The 4th Marquess died in 1870 and his illegitimate son, Richard Wallace, bought Hertford House from his cousin, the 5th Marquess.

The 4th Marquess (left), Madame Oger and Richard Wallace at Bagatelle c.1855

The 4th Marquess bought Bagatelle, the small 18th-century pleasure château in the Bois de Boulogne, in 1835. Madame Oger was one of his mistresses and Wallace acted as his secretary for many years.

A Richard Wallace lived in Paris from the age of 6 and was more French than English. When the siege of Paris by the Prussians ended in 1871, he decided to move to London with his French wife. The Wallaces moved into Hertford House in 1875 after extensive alterations had been carried out. Wallace spent the last three years of his life back at Bagatelle, leaving his wife alone in Hertford House. He died at Bagatelle in 1890 in the same room and the same bed in which the 4th Marquess had died. He left everything to his wife. Lady Wallace continued to live in seclusion in Hertford House until her death seven years later.

The state rooms were the grandest rooms in the house. Unlike the private family apartments, they had a public function. Here the most important visitors were received. The walls of the Front State Room are panelled with crimson silk in gilded frames, a re-creation of the decoration at the end of the 19th century.

There are many Hertford family portraits in this room. Here is a family tree:

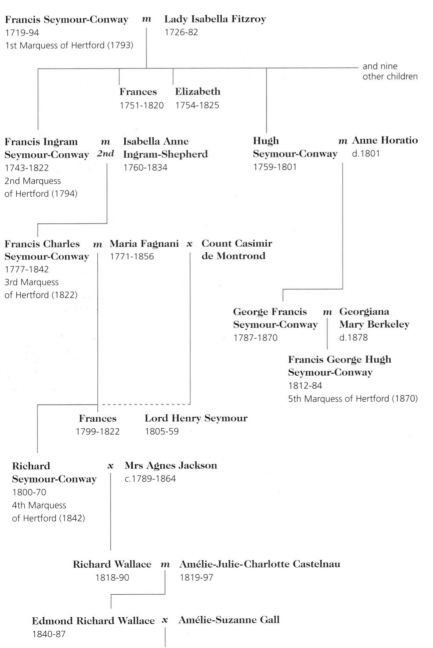

Francis Seymour-Conway *m* Lady Isabella Fitzroy
1719-94   1726-82
1st Marquess of Hertford (1793)

and nine other children

Frances   Elizabeth
1751-1820   1754-1825

Francis Ingram   *m*   Isabella Anne   Hugh   *m* Anne Horatio
Seymour-Conway *2nd* Ingram-Shepherd   Seymour-Conway   d.1801
1743-1822   1760-1834   1759-1801
2nd Marquess
of Hertford (1794)

Francis Charles *m* Maria Fagnani *x* Count Casimir
Seymour-Conway   1771-1856   de Montrond
1777-1842
3rd Marquess
of Hertford (1822)

George Francis   *m* Georgiana
Seymour-Conway   Mary Berkeley
1787-1870   d.1878

Francis George Hugh
Seymour-Conway
1812-84
5th Marquess of Hertford (1870)

Frances   Lord Henry Seymour
1799-1822   1805-59

Richard   *x* Mrs Agnes Jackson
Seymour-Conway   c.1789-1864
1800-70
4th Marquess
of Hertford (1842)

Richard Wallace *m* Amélie-Julie-Charlotte Castelnau
1818-90   1819-97

Edmond Richard Wallace *x* Amélie-Suzanne Gall
1840-87

Four children

Henry Edridge *Isabella, Lady Beauchamp, later 2nd Marchioness of Hertford* 1776-93 (Wallace Collection Archives)

Lord Henry Seymour 1841 (Wallace Collection Archives)

The Marquess of Hertford's eldest son is called the Earl of Yarmouth. His eldest grandson is called Viscount Beauchamp. When the Marquess dies, his son and grandson move up a rank. 'Marquess', 'Earl' and 'Viscount' are all frequently described as 'Lord' and their wives as 'Lady'.

When Francis Seymour-Conway was born in 1719, the Seymour-Conways were a rich family with estates in Warwickshire and Ireland. Their lineage is traced back to Edward Seymour, Earl of Hertford, who was the brother of Jane Seymour, one of Henry VIII's wives. Edward VI, son of Jane Seymour, ascended the throne in 1547 aged 9. Edward Seymour, who had been one of Henry VIII's leading councillors, declared himself Protector of the boy King and the Realm.

The British kings and queens who reigned whilst the Wallace Collection was being formed were George III (1760), George IV (1820), William IV (1830) and Victoria (1837). Royal portraits were displayed by Sir Richard Wallace in the Front State Room as they are today.

Joshua Reynolds *Lady Elizabeth Seymour-Conway*
English 1784 (60.7 x 46.5cm)

Joshua Reynolds *Frances, Countess of Lincoln*
English 1784 (60.7 x 46.5cm)

The 1st Marquess commissioned Reynolds to paint his daughters, Elizabeth and Frances. Elizabeth never married; Frances married Henry, Earl of Lincoln, in 1775.

Thomas Lawrence *The 3rd Marquess of Hertford*
English *c.*1823 (127 x 100.3cm) (on loan from the
National Gallery of Art, Washington DC)

John Hoppner *George IV as Prince of Wales*
English 1792 (126.5 x 100.4cm)

The 3rd Marquess was in his middle forties when his portrait was painted by Lawrence. He had bright red hair and, when he was Lord Yarmouth, was nick-named 'Red Herrings' after the fishing town of Yarmouth in Norfolk.

George IV as Prince of Wales portrays the Prince aged 30. He was a profligate rake known to his friends as 'Prinny'. He showed great favour to Lord Yarmouth and, in 1811, gave him this portrait.

 At the age of 21 Lord Yarmouth (later 3rd Marquess) married Maria Fagnani, known as 'Mie-Mie', the illegitimate daughter of an Italian dancer and the 4th Duke of Queensberry. George Selwyn also believed he was Mie-Mie's father and both men left her considerable fortunes. However, Mie-Mie was not made to feel welcome by her parents-in-law and, after visiting Paris with her husband, remained there with their two small children, Richard and Frances.

In 1803 Lord Yarmouth tried to fetch her back but the war between France and England had recommenced. He was seized as an enemy alien and interned at Verdun. In 1805 Mie-Mie, still in Paris, gave birth to Lord Henry Seymour, generally believed to be the son of Count Casimir de Montrond. Later that year Lord Yarmouth was released and left for London without his wife, a separation which proved permanent.

When the Prince of Wales ascended the throne in 1820, he instituted divorce proceedings against Queen Caroline. She had a great deal of popular support and, on 10 June 1820, the *New Times* reported a mob demanding that households 'illuminate for the Queen this evening!' 'The mob also proceeded to the Marquis of Hertford's elegant mansion in Manchester Square; and although lights were immediately exhibited, the assailants exclaimed, "that will not do, smash the windows." They did so, broke into the hall, and left this house a complete wreck of their savage fury.'

Thomas Lawrence *Margaret, Countess of Blessington*
English 1822 (91.5 x 67cm)

Margaret, Countess of Blessington is a portrait of Margaret Power, an
Irish beauty who married her second husband, the Earl of Blessington,
in 1818 when she was 21. Four years later she took a lover, Alfred,
comte d'Orsay, who became her constant companion. Lady
Blessington was one of the most celebrated society women of her
time. She held a famous literary salon and was an acquaintance of
Byron, who wrote that her portrait had 'set all London raving.'

The portrait of Queen Victoria
was painted the year after she
ascended the throne. Her long
reign lasted until 1901. Sully,
an American citizen, was
commissioned by an anglophile
society in Philadelphia to paint
a portrait of the Queen. The
Wallace Collection portrait was
commissioned by a London firm
of print publishers who intended
to publish engravings after the
painting. Sully kept a journal in
which he noted his impressions
of the Queen: 'And to sum up
all ... I should say decidedly,
that she is quite pretty.'

Thomas Sully *Queen Victoria* American 1838 (142.5 x 112.5cm)

10

William Robert Symonds *Sir Richard Wallace*
English 1885 (67.6 x 56.2cm)

When Sir Richard Wallace sold
his estate at Sudbourne in Suffolk,
the tenants commissioned a
portrait of him from Symonds,
a locally born artist. Symonds
wrote that Wallace 'never sat, but
always preferred to stand with
one hand resting on the back
of a chair & smoking a cigar.'

Heinrich von Angeli
*The Empress Frederick of Germany
as Crown Princess of Prussia*
German 1882 (71 x 58cm)

The Empress Frederick of Germany was Queen Victoria's eldest daughter and a friend
of Richard Wallace. She visited Hertford House and Wallace kept her portrait in his Study.
When Wallace died, the Empress wrote to her mother, 'He was a most generous and
charitable man, and what a connoisseur of art!'

Presentation to Sir Richard Wallace at Hertford House, 9 August 1886

The group stands on the steps outside the Dining Room in the courtyard of Hertford
House. Sir Richard and Lady Wallace are on the left. Symonds holds the portrait.
Behind Lady Wallace is John Murray Scott, Sir Richard Wallace's secretary.

The Back State Room is a tribute to the patronage of Louis XV and his mistress, Madame de Pompadour. The rococo style, which emerged 1715-35, flourished under their auspices. 'Rococo' derives from 'rocaille', which means loose stones or rocky ground. It is an exuberant, animated style, characterised by rampant sprays of foliage, swirling scrolls and asymmetry.

Antoine-Robert Gaudreaus and Jacques Caffiéri, Commode (chest of drawers) French 1739 (88.8 x 195.5 x 80.6cm)

Try to find a straight line anywhere on the commode and you will be frustrated. This monumental piece was supplied for Louis XV's new bedroom at Versailles. It is decorated with asymmetrical gilt-bronze mounts, made by Caffiéri, which creep and crawl over the curved surface, disregarding the division of drawers. Their flamboyant twists cunningly double up as drawer handles.

Gaudreaus (c.1680-1751) was the leading French cabinet maker in the rococo style. For the last 25 years of his life, he worked exclusively for Louis XV. The commode is one of his masterpieces.

The commode bore silent witness to the death-bed confession of Louis XV. It was inherited by the late King's First Gentleman of the Bedchamber, the duc d'Aumont (one of the perks of the job). Its subsequent fate until 1865 is a mystery. It must have been witness to at least one more key event of French history – the French Revolution. Perhaps this is when its original top of red and grey marble was lost or broken. If only furniture could speak!

12

Jacques Caffiéri
Chandelier, French 1751 (179 x 190cm)

The twelve-light chandelier is made of gilt bronze. It was given by Louis XV to his eldest daughter, Louise-Elisabeth. The strong twisting forms are like plants which have grown wild. Beneath each arm is a posy of flowers with a rose; the candleholders are shaped like vases.

Caffiéri (1673-1755) trained as a sculptor and became the leading metal-founder and chaser of the Louis XV period. He was one of the finest craftsmen of the rococo style in any medium. Once bronze or brass had been cast, the surface was finished by chasing which removed blemishes and refined the detail. Then it was gilded with a mixture of ground gold and mercury.

Attributed to Jean-Claude Duplessis,
Elephant vase, French 1757 (39.3 x 28.5cm)

The Sèvres porcelain elephant vase belongs to a garniture. A pot pourri vase is flanked by a pair of vases '*à tête d'éléphant*'. The elephants have eyebrows and eyelashes, brown eyes and black pupils. They have gilded hairs in their ears and gilded wrinkles on their trunks, which support candleholders. The vases were possibly bought by Madame de Pompadour.

At a time when washing was minimal, pot pourri was used to perfume rooms and mask unpleasant smells. Much French 18th-century interior decoration was inspired by the garden. A pot pourri vase completed the scheme by bringing the scent of flowers indoors.

Garniture of vases, French 1758 (central vase: 48.9 x 29.3cm)

Garniture of vases,
detail of central vase

The Sèvres porcelain garniture of vases was bought by Louis XV when he visited the Sèvres factory in 1759, probably with Madame de Pompadour who chose a tea service. The vases are decorated with military encampments. Notice the green snakes with gilded scales which are entwined on the central vase.

The porcelain in this room is soft-paste porcelain which is particularly fragile in the kiln. Every piece that emerged perfect from the production process was a miracle. First, the raw piece was fired, glazed and fired again. Then it was painted with a 'ground colour' (for example, green, rose or blue), leaving white 'reserves', and fired. The reserves were painted with decoration such as flowers. The enamel colours were often applied one at a time and fired separately at decreasing temperatures. Finally, the piece was gilded with a mixture of powdered gold and adhesive and fired at the lowest temperature.

Musical clock, French c.1762 (90.5 x 66 x 30cm)

The musical clock can play thirteen different tunes including 'Ah! Vous dirai-je, Maman?', known in England as 'Baa, baa, black sheep'. On top of the clock, a spaniel retrieves a game bird. The sporting theme is continued by the French hunting horn on the right. The instruments rest on books of sheet music. The design of the clock case is ascribed to Duplessis.

Jean-Baptiste Oudry *The Dead Roe* French 1721 (193 x 260cm)   Jean-Baptiste Oudry *The Dead Wolf* French 1721 (193 x 260cm)

The Dead Roe and *The Dead Wolf* are the masterpieces of Oudry's
early career. They would probably have hung in a room used for
dining. Animals killed in the hunt, fruit gathered from the land and
a tempting *pâté en croûte* decorated with *fleurs de lis*, the French
royal emblem, are displayed in monumental settings. The comic dog
taunted by an escaped pheasant is a typical playful touch. Oudry's
palette favours whites, pale blues, pinks, blue-greens and greys. The
effect is mouth-watering. Who could resist the plump figs cooling in
the porcelain bowl placed in the stream?

Beauvais tapestry seat cover (on sofa), detail, French c.1755

The tapestry cover depicts animal scenes after Oudry. On the seat,
a stag is pursued by two hounds. The royal Beauvais factory was
founded under Louis XIV, and Oudry became chief designer in
1726. His hunting subjects and rococo palette were perfectly
suited to textile design.

Shooting party at Sudbourn c.1873

Lady Wallace is being helped out of the carriage on the left. Sir Richard Wallace is standing to the right of the luncheon table. Sir Richard and Lady Wallace held regular shooting parties on their estate in Suffolk.

Astronomical clock
French c.1750 (294.5 x 133.5 x 91cm)

The astronomical clock is an 18th-century example of 'toys for boys'. It was made for Jean Paris de Monmartel, Banker to the Court of Louis XV, who was no doubt delighted by its comprehensive and incredibly complicated system of telling the time. If you know where to look, you can find the time in hours, minutes and seconds, solar time (like that you read on a sun dial) in hours and minutes, the sign of the Zodiac, the date, the day of the week, the time at any place in the northern hemisphere, the age of the moon and its current phase, and the position of the sun in the sky, or the moon if it is night.

Attributed to Jean-Claude Duplessis, Toilet service, French 1763 (powder box: 10.2 x 13.3cm)

A toilet service was displayed with a mirror on a dressing table and was usually draped with fabric, such as *toile* (hence 'toilette'). The toilette was a public event: Madame de Pompadour was dressed, made up, bewigged, powdered and bejewelled in front of an audience of ambassadors, bishops, courtiers, friends and tradesmen. There was a formal seating arrangement and less important visitors had to stand.

The toilet service is made of Sèvres porcelain. The powder box (large) was for wig or hair powder made of scented starch. A silk powder puff sat inside and gold mounts kept mites out. The pomade pot (tall) contained heavy hair grease made from apples (hence 'pomade') and goat's fat. The patch box (small) was for fashionable, black face-patches of velvet or taffeta, which were glued to the skin. The large brush is a clothes brush; the smaller is a whisk for dusting wig powder from the shoulders.

Inkstand, detail

Jean-Claude Duplessis, Inkstand, French 1758 (17 x 38 x 27.1cm)

Duplessis (d.1774) was multi-talented. He worked as a goldsmith, a sculptor and a founder and chaser of metal. In the 1750s, he worked as a designer at the Sèvres factory and probably designed all the porcelain shapes made before 1763 which are in this room.

The Sèvres porcelain inkstand was given by Louis XV to his daughter, Marie-Adélaïde. On the right a terrestrial globe represents the world as known in 1758. This held the inkwell. On the left a celestial globe is painted with the signs of the Zodiac. This held a sand-shaker. When the cover of the celestial globe was closed, the silver-gilt[†] sand-shaker shone through the pierced stars making them twinkle in the candlelight. Beneath the French royal crown in the centre was a sponge for wiping your pen nib. Pens were laid in the tray and there was a bell inside the crown. Having written her letter, dried the ink with sand and wiped her pen, Marie-Adélaïde could ring the bell and summon a servant to deliver the letter.

In 1756 the Vincennes porcelain factory moved to Sèvres, near Madame de Pompadour's château at Bellevue – she wished to encourage the King's interest in the factory and three years later he became the sole proprietor. The factory had the exclusive right to produce any kind of white porcelain. It survived the French Revolution and was nationalised in 1793.

I n the Dining Room you can compare portraits of four aristocratic French women of the *ancien régime*. Two of them were victims of the Terror of the French Revolution.

The Dining Room, c. 1890

Jean-Marc Nattier *The comtesse de Tillières* French 1750 (80 x 63cm)

Jean-Marc Nattier *The marquise de Belestat* French 1755 (81 x 64cm)

The comtesse de Tillières is an example of a new type of informal portrait in French painting which aimed, above all, at 'naturalness'. The comtesse wears a simple powdered coiffure. Her natural expression and her relaxed seated pose give the portrait an air of intimacy.

Nattier's portrait of the marquise de Belestat takes a very different approach. The marquise was a lady-in-waiting to the daughters of Louis XV, including Mesdames Victoire and Marie-Adélaïde. She attended the Court at Versailles in 1754 and 1755. She is shown in the formal *robe à la française*, three-quarter length, without hands and in front of a neutral background. The composition and style of the painting was a formula repeated by Nattier many times for formal portraits of fashionable ladies of the Court. Nattier's objective was to show how closely the sitter's appearance conformed to the current ideals of female beauty rather than to represent her personality.

Louis XV had seven daughters. He sent four of them, including the 5 year old Victoire, away from Court for their upbringing because they were too expensive to maintain. The 6 year old Marie-Adélaïde was supposed to go but she clung to her father in tears, begging to stay, and he repented.

Jean-Antoine Houdon *Madame Victoire de France*
French 1777 (78.8cm high)

Jean-Antoine Houdon *Madame de Sérilly*
French 1782 (62cm high)

Madame Victoire was the fifth daughter of Louis XV. The bust is probably a faithful representation of the 44 year old Princess. She lived her life at Court in the company of her unmarried sister, Marie-Adélaïde. In 1791 the Princesses fled from France and took refuge in Italy. In 1799 they were on the move again but severe winter travelling conditions proved fatal and they both died at Trieste.

Madame de Sérilly was aged 19 when her portrait bust was made. She was a maid of honour to Marie-Antoinette and a devoted friend of Louis XVI's sister, Madame Elisabeth. Her husband held office at Court and, when the Revolution started, they retired to the country. In 1794 they were accused of plotting with Madame Elisabeth to assist Louis XVI (who was by then dead). Madame Elisabeth declared falsely that Madame de Sérilly was pregnant and, as a result, Madame de Sérilly escaped the guillotine.

Houdon (1741-1828) was the foremost French sculptor of the second half of the 18th century and one of the most outstanding portrait sculptors of all time. He is best known for his remarkably vivid portrait busts. After the Revolution he continued working but gradually fell out of favour.

The storming of the Bastille on 14 July 1789 is usually regarded as the beginning of the French Revolution. Louis XVI was forced to accept the power of the National Assembly and a constitutional monarchy. This lasted until August 1792 when a more radical phase began. A centralised authoritarian government ruled through the Committee of Public Safety which instituted the Terror. Thousands of people were guillotined for crimes against the Revolution. Louis XVI was executed on 21 January 1793, and Marie-Antoinette on 12 October in the same year.

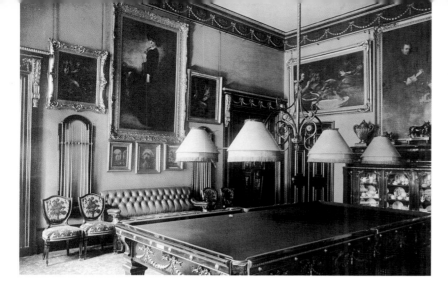

The Billiard Room, c.1890

During the reign of Louis XIV, the self-styled Sun King, France became pre-eminent in the arts and gained her reputation for fine craftsmanship. The most talented artists of the day were brought together to promote the power and magnificence of the monarchy. The King's most influential minister was Colbert, who achieved cultural control through the Academies and Court patronage.

François Lemoyne *Perseus and Andromeda*
French 1723 (183 x 149.7cm)

The subject of *Perseus and Andromeda* is taken from Ovid's *Metamorphoses*.[†] Andromeda is chained to a rock as a sacrifice to a sea-monster. Her parents and other anguished onlookers stand on the shore in the distance. Perseus, flying overhead, sees the beautiful girl and falls in love. He swoops down to slay the monster and rescue Andromeda. Lemoyne's elegant, colourful style had a profound influence on the development of history painting in 18th-century France. Boucher was one of his pupils.

French School *Madame de Ventadour with portraits of Louis XIV and his heirs*
c.1715-20 (127.6 x 161cm)

Madame de Ventadour inherited the post of Governess to the Royal
Children from her mother. She leads the infant Louis XV, then the
duc d'Anjou. Louis XIV, seated in the centre, points to his heir.
Louis, the Grand Dauphin, rests his arm on the back of the chair.
His son, Louis, the duc de Bourgogne, stands to the right. Behind
the group are a pair of busts on pedestals. Henri IV is on the left and
Louis XIII is on the right. The heads of Louis XIII, XIV and XV are
carefully aligned. The painted scene on the wall behind represents
Apollo, the sun god, a reference to Louis XIV, the Sun King. The
ages of the men portrayed are inconsistent. They are copied from
the best-known portraits painted during their lifetimes.

In 1712 there was
an epidemic of measles.
Madame de Ventadour hid
the 2 year old duc d'Anjou
from the royal doctors
and was thus credited with
saving the life of Louis XIV's
only surviving male heir.
(The doctors' treatments
had failed to save Louis XV's
parents and elder brother.)
The painting celebrates
Madame de Ventadour's
role in saving the
Bourbon dynasty.

The gilt-bronze† *Marly Horses*
are reduced replicas of marbles
by Coustou which were installed
in 1745 by the horse pond in
the park at Marly, the royal
pleasure house. In 1794 they
were removed to the entrance
of the Champs-Elysées in Paris,
where they acquired iconic status
as 'La gloire de France'. The
brute powers of man and beast
are pitched against each other
as the nude male figures strive
to control the rearing horses.

After Guillaume Coustou the Elder *The Marly Horses* French c.1805 (59.8 and 58.4cm high)

Charles Le Brun was First Painter to the King. He was a founder of the French Royal Academy of Painting and Sculpture and a director of the Gobelins factory, established by Colbert to provide furnishings for the royal residences. Together with the architect Louis Le Vau and the garden designer André Le Nôtre, he transformed Louis XIV's hunting lodge at Versailles.

Antoine Coyzevox *Charles Le Brun* French 1676
(66cm high)

The bust of Charles Le Brun is a model made of terracotta, a sensitive medium which lent itself to Coyzevox's genius. He has captured brilliantly the nuances and subtleties of facial expression. Le Brun is shown as a fellow artist in an informal pose. The medallion at his neck was given to him by Louis XIV. Coyzevox made a marble bust of this model which he offered as his reception piece to the French Royal Academy of Painting and Sculpture in 1679, the year that Le Brun became President.

Terracotta models are analogous to drawings or *modelli* prepared for paintings. They are valued for a spontaneity and verve which can be lost in the more laborious process of casting bronze or carving stone.

Antoine Coyzevox *Louis XIV* French c. 1699
(74.9cm high)

The bronze bust of Louis XIV shows the king towards the end of his life. He wears a full-bottomed wig and a lace cravat. His armour is decorated with *fleurs de lis*, the emblem of the French kings. Coyzevox was appointed Sculptor to the King in 1667.

The Bourbon dynasty
of Kings of France

Henri IV (1553-1610)
King 1589
m. Maria de' Medici

|

Louis XIII (1601-43)
(eldest son of Henri IV)
King 1610

|

Louis XIV (1638-1715)
(only legitimate son
of Louis XIII)
King 1643

|

Louis, the Grand Dauphin
(1661-1711)
(eldest son of Louis XIV)

|

Louis, duc de Bourgogne
(1682-1712)
(eldest son of the Grand
Dauphin)

|

Louis XV (1710-74)
duc d'Anjou
(3rd son of
the duc de Bourgogne,
great-grandson of Louis XIV)
King 1715, aged 5

|

Louis, the Dauphin (1729-65)
(only son of Louis XV)

|

Louis XVI (1754-93)
(2nd son of the Dauphin,
grandson of Louis XV)
King 1774

André-Charles Boulle, Wardrobe, French 1715 (311.5 x 196 x 65.8cm)

Boulle (1642-1732) was the first great French cabinet maker. He became Cabinet Maker to the King in 1672, on the recommendation of Colbert. He had lodgings in the Louvre and was thus exempted from guild regulations which forbade cabinet makers from working in both metal and wood.

The wardrobe is veneered with *contre-partie* Boulle marquetry. The use of metal, mother-of-pearl, horn and precious stones in the decoration of furniture was introduced to France in the 17th century by Italian craftsmen. Boulle developed this technique and gave his name to a type of marquetry. He used brass and turtleshell in elaborate designs embellished with gilt-bronze mounts of outstanding quality.

Sheets of turtleshell and brass are glued together and the design cut out with a special saw. Once cut, the layers can be combined to produce either a shell ground with a brass design (*première-partie*) or a brass ground with a shell design (*contre-partie*). *Première-partie* was more expensive than *contre-partie* because turtleshell was more expensive than brass. The brass was often engraved and black pigment rubbed into the engraved lines.

Attributed to André-Charles Boulle
Cabinet on stand, French
c.1665-70 (186.7 x 123 x 65cm)

The cabinet shows the development of Boulle's technique. It includes marquetry of exotic woods, which Boulle used during the early part of his career, and areas of marquetry using metal. The top drawers on each side are veneered with *fleurs de lis* and other motifs in pewter, brass and copper against a ground of ebony.[†]

In the Louis XIV period, a cabinet was generally the most elaborate piece of furniture in the house; the term 'cabinet maker' came to be applied to superior types of joiner from the 1680s. A cabinet consisted of a case of small drawers and compartments intended for the storage and display of precious objects, for example a collection of medals or jewels.

Inkstand, French 1710 (19 x 55.8 x 38.6cm)

The centre of the inkstand shows the coat of arms of the guild of Barber-Surgeons. Three drug jars surround a *fleur de lis*. The motto above translates 'by knowledge and by manual skill.' On a band around the top of the inkstand are the names of twelve members of the guild. The first is Georgius Mareschal, who operated on Louis XIV's physician to remove gall stones and then became First Surgeon to the King. There are two inkwells, with circular lids, and two sand boxes, which have lids pierced with *fleurs de lis*.

At the time the inkstand was made, surgeons, unlike physicians, were regarded as artisans rather than intellectuals. Like painters, they strove to achieve the status of an academic profession; the inkstand is a statement of their aspirations. In 1731 they succeeded in becoming an Academy of Surgery.

Richard Wallace lived most of his life in mid 19th-century Paris, a city still recovering from the Terror of the French Revolution and the collapse of the Napoleonic empire. Writers, artists and collectors harked back to medieval tales and 16th-century French history for their inspiration. The Sixteenth-Century Gallery and the Smoking Room beyond reflect Wallace's 19th-century romantic taste for medieval and renaissance treasures.

Giovanni Battista Cima da Conegliano
St Catherine of Alexandria and *The Virgin and Child with St Francis and St Anthony of Padua*
Italian 1502 (193.2 x 84.9cm)

St Catherine stands with a palm leaf, the symbol of Christian martyrdom. The Roman Emperor Maxentius sentenced fifty Christian converts to death and Catherine, herself a convert, tried to intervene on their behalf. Maxentius tried to punish her by tying her to a spiked wheel, but a thunderbolt from heaven destroyed it before it could harm her so he beheaded her with a sword. You can see a fragment of the wheel behind her. Her iconic status is emphasised by the architectural canopy and the pedestal upon which she stands like a living statue. *St Catherine* originally formed part of an altarpiece in Mestre, near Venice, with the lunette, *The Virgin and Child with St Francis and St Anthony of Padua*, above.

Germain Pilon *Charles IX*
French c.1575 (62.2 high)

Youth
probably Italian, early 17th century
(10 x 7.5cm)

Age
probably Italian, early 17th century
(10 x 7.5cm)

Charles IX was one of France's least distinguished kings. His weak chin and sideways glance reveal his vacillating and ineffectual nature. Pilon was one of the greatest French sculptors of the 16th century. His brilliant portraits had considerable influence on those who came after him.

Youth and *Age* are small wax sculptures. Youth is a plump girl who squeezes her left breast between her fingers. Age is a skinny, wrinkled hag with sagging breasts who holds a crutch. The pair function as a *vanitas*[†] warning: there is no point in dressing your hair with jewels and decorating your body with necklaces and bracelets when your flesh is sure to shrivel and pearls are of no use in Hell.

Waxes were first made in the early 16th century, most commonly as portraits. Their ability to imitate the characteristics of flesh can be both fascinating and repellent. The effect is often enhanced by the addition of real hair, textiles and paste gems.

Barthélemy Prieur *Mother and Child*
French c.1600 (14.6cm high)

The bronze group, *Mother and Child*, is a surprising combination of an idealised figure, as favoured by Italian renaissance artists, and everyday subject matter, more typical of the northern tradition. A mother, who is nude and resembles a classical statue, helps her child, who wears a shirt, to urinate. The bronze is finely detailed and was embellished with a translucent red-gold lacquer.[†]

The primary method for casting bronze sculpture in the 16th and 17th centuries was the lost-wax method. In brief, a wax model of the sculpture was set in clay and, using a complicated technique, the wax was melted and replaced with molten bronze which solidified into the shape previously occupied by the model. The clay was broken away and the surface of the bronze figure tidied up and finished by various techniques of 'cold' working, such as chasing.[†]

Pieter Pourbus *An Allegory of True Love* Flemish c.1547 (132.8 x 205.7cm)

In *An Allegory of True Love*, a winged Cupid, on the left, and a Jester, on the right, warn of the folly of carnal love. In the centre, Wisdom embraces Fidelity, who points at the table laden with the food of love. The other mythological and allegorical characters are arranged in four groups of three, each consisting of a famous classical lover embracing one of the Graces but distracted by a female figure symbolising, from left to right, inconstancy, superficial emotion, fickleness, and luxury and excess.

Standing salt and cover
English 1578 (30.6cm high)

The silver-gilt† standing salt was made in Elizabethan London. Salt was kept beneath the cover on a recess at the top of the drum-shape. The decoration, which includes lions' heads and bunches of grapes, was made by hammering the drum from the back and then chasing the surface. A Roman soldier stands on top of the cover with a spear in his hand.

Salt was a rare, necessary and valuable commodity in the Renaissance. Table wares for salt ('salts') became ceremonial objects whose size was out of all proportion to the small amount of salt which they contained. A salt was used to mark the place of the highest-ranking person at the table.

Attributed to the Master of Coëtivy
Boethius instructed by Philosophy French c.1460-70 (24.1 x 16.5cm)

Boethius instructed by Philosophy is the frontispiece
to Book II of a French translation of Boethius' celebrated
On the Consolations of Philosophy, written in early 6th
century Rome. Boethius listens to Philosophy, who holds
a book and a rod. The walls of the room are covered with
tapestry hangings and the windows open to a view of the
town. Outside, Fortune turns her wheel: at the top is a
king; on the left a prosperous and smug-looking man is
on the way up; opposite him another man is on the way
down and at the bottom a king is falling off the wheel.

Illuminated manuscript cuttings are pages from Choir Books and Books of
Hours dating from the Middle Ages and the Renaissance. The mutilation of
manuscript books for their initials and miniatures was not uncommon in the
18th and 19th centuries.

Martial Courteys, Platter *Apollo and the Muses* French c.1580 (56.3 x 41.7cm)

The platter is a Limoges painted enamel. Apollo, the sun god, plays
a viol on Mount Helicon, home of the nine Muses, the goddesses of
creative inspiration. The Muses play different instruments including
an organ, a tambourine, cymbals and a triangle. Behind them are
two poets. The winged horse, Pegasus, stamps his foot, causing the
Hippocrene stream, the source of poetic inspiration, to spring forth.
You can see Hippocrene below, pouring her spring water from an urn.

The town of Limoges in
France was renowned in the
16th century for its painted
enamels. Enamel was fired
on to a metal base. Different
colours were heated to
different temperatures in the
kiln and for varying periods
of time in order for the
components to fuse together
to just the right degree. Some
of the Muses' dresses have
been given an iridescent
quality by laying foil under
translucent enamel.

Wine glass, Venetian, late 16th century
(18.3 x 8.9cm)

The bowl of the wine glass is
made of ice-glass (glass made
to look like ice), which was
very fashionable from the
mid 16th century.

The ewer is made of clear,
colourless glass incorporating
opaque white canes of glass
which are arranged in a pattern
imitating lace. The molten glass
was blown into a mould to achieve
the square projections. The
handle is decorated with simple
parallel lines of white canes.

Ewer, Venetian, late 16th century (27.1 x 13cm)

There were glassmakers in
Venice as early as the 7th
century. The art of making
clear, almost colourless
'crystal' glass was discovered
in Venice in the 15th century
and soon Venetian workshops
were supplying Europe with
wine glasses and dishes
of an unsurpassed lightness
and delicacy. The pieces
were formed from semi-
molten glass gathered
on the end of a blow-pipe,
inflated and worked
between the blow-pipe and
an iron rod. The glass was
regularly reheated at the
furnace during the process.

Pietro Torrigiano *Bust of Christ* Italian
c.1515 (45.8 x 96.5cm)

The marble bust of Christ came
originally from Westminster
Abbey. Torrigiano, who studied
in Florence with Michelangelo,
came to England and worked for
Henry VIII.

Sir Richard Wallace would have invited his male guests to the Smoking Room after dinner to discuss the affairs of the day over an enjoyable pipe or cigar. The walls were lined with tiles decorated in the Turkish style, made by the Minton factory in Stoke-on-Trent, and the floor was laid with a patterned mosaic. The sumptuous oriental interior was a highly fashionable look for a late Victorian smoking room. Today it exhibits medieval and renaissance works of art.

Minton tiles, c.1872-5

Before the Wallaces moved into Hertford House in 1875, they undertook extensive alterations. The east and west wings, including the Smoking Room and galleries on the first floor, were added to the 18th-century part of the house; the courtyard was created in the centre and the Great Gallery was built above the stables and coach house. The building was given the red brick façade which it has today. During the three years that it took to complete the alterations, a large part of the collection was lent to the newly established Bethnal Green Museum. The exhibition attracted five million visitors and contributed to the growing fame of Sir Richard Wallace.

Richard Dighton *Sir Richard Wallace* c.1873 (Wallace Collection Archives)

Richard Jackson was born in London, the son of Mrs Agnes Jackson and Lord Beauchamp (later 4th Marquess), who was ten years Mrs Jackson's junior. When Richard was six, his mother took him to Paris to find his father, who took the boy and gave him to his grandmother, the 3rd Marchioness. When he was 20, Richard began an affair with Amélie-Julie Castelnau who was working in a perfumer's shop. She bore him an illegitimate son, Edmond Richard, in 1840. Two years later, Richard had himself baptised Richard Wallace (Mrs Jackson's maiden name). Wallace and Amélie-Julie were eventually married nearly thirty years later in 1871, after the 4th Marquess died. Evidently, the 4th Marquess did not approve of the match.

The Crucifixion French c.1300 (26.6cm high)

The Crucifixion is the central leaf of an ivory triptych[†] which would have been for private devotional use. It was carved in Paris, the centre of ivory carving in the medieval period. Christ is crucified between the two thieves. Above Him, angels hold the moon and the sun. The figures have been deeply undercut and the expressive details of their heads are quite remarkable.

Bernardino Luini *The Virgin and Child in a Landscape* Italian, early 16th century (73.2 x 45.4cm)

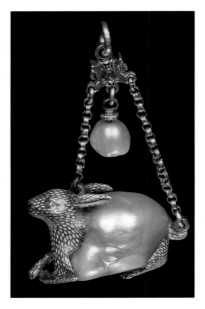

Hare pendant, German, late 16th century (3.2cm long)

The exquisite hare pendant is made from an irregularly shaped pearl mounted with gold. The gold is chased[†] and decorated with flecks of white enamel to create the realistic details of head, ears, paws and tail. In the 16th century, jewellery became an essential accessory for the very rich as dress fashion grew more ostentatious.

The Virgin is depicted with downcast eyes in the traditional attitude of humility. Her sweet face, the rocky niche in which she sits and the luminescent landscape beyond show the influence of Leonardo da Vinci. The objects on the red marble ledge in the foreground refer to Christ's divinity and His future Passion. The book is a symbol of Christ's innate wisdom; the ivory teething stick with black ribbons recalls His innocence and suffering; the white sheet is a harbinger of the winding sheet in which His dead body will be wrapped.

After Alessandro Algardi
Jupiter Victorious over the Titans
French or Italian c.1650-89 (127cm high)

After Alessandro Algardi
Juno Controlling the Winds
French or Italian c.1650-89 (125.8cm high)

Jupiter, seated on his eagle and holding his thunderbolt, represents Fire. The king of the gods has defeated the rebellious Titans who crouch beneath him, crushed by rocks. Juno, seated on her peacock, symbolises Air. The queen of the gods has defeated three hostile Winds by trapping them in a cave. Notice their puffed cheeks. Algardi, second only to Bernini amongst Italian sculptors of the mid 17th century, sculpted a set of four fire-dogs representing the Elements for Philip IV, King of Spain. The Wallace bronzes derive from Algardi's models. They belonged to the Grand Dauphin, Louis XIV's son, and passed into the French royal collection where they were amongst the most valuable of over 300 bronzes.

Bell of St Mura, Irish, 11th century and later (15.8 x 8.95 x 7.7cm)

The hand bell is reputed to have come from the Abbey of Fahan, County Donegal, Ireland, founded by St Mura in the 7th century. The bronze body of the bell was probably made at Kells, County Meath, the great centre of art and monastic life. The decoration was applied to the venerated object in stages. The earliest is an Irish style of Viking ornament seen in the bottom right corner where a later piece has become detached. The silver filigree and cast plaques, and the rock crystal and amber stones were added in the 13th-16th centuries. For hundreds of years the bell was valued for its power to alleviate human suffering. However, its last keeper was destitute and had to sell it.

Wine-cooler, Italian 1574 (40 x 62 x 71cm)

Dish, Italian 1500-25 (38.9cm)

The maiolica wine-cooler would have been placed on the table or on the floor during banquets. It was filled with water, snow or ice to keep flasks of wine cool. Monsters with human heads and rippling muscles support the tremendous weight of the bowl. They have flippers for hands, the legs of a lion and the wings and tail of a dragon. Inside the bowl a sea battle rages. The outside of the bowl and the inner border are decorated with grotesques.[†] The wine-cooler was made in Urbino for Cosimo de' Medici,[†] one of the greatest patrons of the arts of all time.

The dish, which was made in Deruta, shows the profile of a young girl. A medallion with a portrait of her lover hangs from her neck. The scroll is inscribed, '*Sola speranza el mio cor tene*' ('My heart has only hope').

Hispano-Moresque ceramics and Italian maiolica are made from tin-glazed earthenware.[†] First, an undecorated earthenware piece is fired in the kiln. Then it is coated with an opaque white, tin-oxide based glaze. It is decorated with coloured pigments derived from metallic oxides. The colours are absorbed into the glaze as soon as they are applied and so corrections are not possible. The piece is given a second firing which fixes the glaze and decoration and gives it a glossy surface. The technique was developed in Baghdad in the 9th century in an attempt to rival white Chinese porcelain. From there it passed to southern Spain, where Hispano-Moresque ceramics were made under Arab influence in the second half of the 14th and the 15th centuries, and thence to Italy.

Dish, Italian 1525 (44.6cm)

The maiolica dish depicts fifteen beautiful maidens bathing in a pool decorated with grotesques. In the background are a lake and a castle. You may notice that the silver and red areas of decoration are lustred: they glisten when caught by the light. The dish was made in Gubbio in Master Giorgio Andreoli's workshop, famous for its lustred wares.

Maiolica painters used engravings as inspiration for their decorations. They often combined elements from more than one engraving and the same detail might be used in a different context on a number of pieces. The maidens on the dish divide into three groups, each of which is derived from a different engraving.

Bernard Palissy, Oval dish
French 1580s (49.3 x 37.1cm)

A grass snake wriggles along Palissy's earthenware dish which is painted with lead glaze. A pike and a smaller fish swim in a swiftly flowing stream which surrounds an island of pebbles in the centre. Crayfish, a lizard and a frog lurk on the rim of the dish. Palissy used plaster moulds of the creatures, which were made from real specimens.

Lustred ware is tin-glazed earthenware painted in certain areas with an additional glaze containing a small amount of silver oxide, to achieve yellow lustre, or copper oxide, to achieve red lustre, and fired for a third time in a special, smaller kiln. One contemporary wrote, 'The art is so uncertain that often out of a hundred pieces of ware hardly six are good. When wares are good they are paid for in gold.'

A brilliant generation of French painters came to maturity in the 1820s. France was scarred by thirty years of turbulence culminating in her defeat at the Battle of Waterloo and the collapse of the Napoleonic Empire. Painters began to search for the origins of modern morality and culture in post-classical history.

Paul Delaroche *The State Barge of Cardinal Richelieu on the Rhône*
French 1829 (56.4 x 97.5cm)

Paul Delaroche *Cardinal Mazarin's Last Sickness*
French 1830 (57.2 x 97.3cm)

The pair of paintings by Delaroche, who was willing to bend the facts of history in order to evoke more effectively the spirit of the time, show the dying moments of the two cardinals who dominated French history during the first half of the 17th century.

The State Barge shows Cardinal Richelieu, Louis XIII's chief minister, travelling up the Rhône. He tows the marquis de Cinq-Mars and François-Auguste de Thou, guarded by soldiers with halberds, in a smaller boat behind. The prisoners had conspired to overthrow the Cardinal and, though mortally ill, he was determined to escort them to Lyons for their execution. He died less than three months later. The sheer extravagance of Richelieu's silk-draped barge is emphasised by the rich oriental carpet which trails in the water.

The Last Sickness shows Cardinal Mazarin on his deathbed. He was chief minister during the minority of Louis XIV and rose to a position of wealth and power equalled only by his predecessor, Richelieu. Card players sit at a gaming table by Mazarin's bed and his niece plays his card for him. The Spanish Ambassador, a solemn man in black, bows to the Cardinal. The room hums with gossip and intrigue.

 Cardinals Richelieu and Mazarin were characterised by the writer, Voltaire:[†] 'the mind of Richelieu breathed fire and revenge, while Mazarin was prudent, cunning and eager for wealth.'

Delacroix's painting shows the execution in 1355 of Marino Faliero, Doge of Venice, punished for conspiring against the Venetian state. The subject is taken from a tragic poem by Byron, published in 1820. The decapitated body of Faliero lies at the foot of the stairs. At the top, a Venetian senator holds aloft the instrument of death, a bloody sword. The figures are dressed in 16th-century costume despite the 14th-century tale. Some are derived from paintings by Venetian renaissance artists. *The Execution* was painted while Delacroix was sharing a Paris studio with his friend, Bonington.

Ferdinand-Victor-Eugène Delacroix *The Execution of the Doge Marino Faliero*
French 1825-6 (145.6 x 113.8cm)

Henri IV and the Spanish Ambassador depicts an anecdote from the life of Henri IV, King of France 1589-1610. He plays piggy-back with his children watched by Queen Marie de Médicis. The Spanish Ambassador, standing on the right, is clearly startled by the want of kingly behaviour. Bonington has based the faces of the King and Queen on historical portraits. His approach to history painting was more light-hearted than that of many of his French contemporaries.

Richard Parkes Bonington *Henri IV and the Spanish Ambassador*
English 1827-8 (38.4 x 52.4cm)

Lady Wallace's housekeeper was Mrs Jane Buckley, a Londoner by birth. She was 'very motherly and easily "got round" by the servants.' There were over thirty servants including housemaids, kitchen maids, a lady's maid, a butler, footmen, a valet, coachmen, a groom and stable lads.

Trophies of arms and armour from India, the Middle East, the lands of the old Ottoman Empire and the Far East pattern the walls of the Oriental Armoury. Sir Richard Wallace regarded his armouries as part of the art collection and displayed them accordingly.

The Oriental Armoury c.1890

A The Oriental Armoury was largely collected by the 4th Marquess in the last decade of his life. He was more interested in the exotic decorative appeal of the armour and weapons than their history. It was the height of fashion in the 1860s to decorate one's smoking room or study with oriental armour.

The Indian dagger is one of the finest in the world. It was made for a nobleman at the court of the Mughal Emperor in India, or possibly for the Emperor himself, either Jahangir, or his son, Shah Jahan. It has a solid-gold hilt[†] set with diamonds and flowers of rubies with emerald leaves.

The Persian dagger is one of the earliest and most beautiful examples of its kind. The hilt is carved from jade and inlaid with gold. The blade is decorated with jackals and hares frolicking amidst arabesques[†] and lotus blossoms. The maker has signed and dated his work.

Dagger, Indian, early 17th century
(36cm long (without scabbard)) [OA1409]

Dagger, Persian 1496-7
(34cm long) [OA1414]

Ceremonial mace, Indian, late 18th century (77.5cm long) [OA1760]

Tipu Sultan, the 'Tiger of Mysore', was ruler of the independent kingdom of Mysore, in southern India, at the end of the 18th century. He was fascinated by the beauty and deadly power of tigers; representations of tigers and tiger-stripes adorned his palaces, weapons and clothes. The soldiers of the British East India Company stormed his palace-fortress of Seringapathan in 1799 and the Tiger of Mysore was killed in the thick of the fighting.

Tipu Sultan's tulwar, Indian late 18th century (89cm long) [OA1402]

The fine silver-gilt† tiger-headed Indian ceremonial mace ('sota') is one of a pair. The tiger's tongue protrudes from its open mouth, which is lined with teeth. Its eyes are set with garnets. Sotas were carried in processions by officials heralding the arrival of an important person.

The Indian tulwar† is inscribed on the blade in gold 'the personal shamshir of Tipu Sultan'. The hilt is made of carved jade inlaid with gold and set with rubies, emeralds and diamonds. The blade dates from the 16th century: a fine blade was highly prized and often mounted in a new hilt. The Sultan's badge, a gold tiger, was probably applied when the blade was remounted.

In the late 15th century, central and western Persia (present-day Iran) were ruled by Uzun Hasan, the leader of the Ak Kuyun Turkoman tribe. Sultan Hosain Mirza reigned in Herat, eastern Persia (present-day Afghanistan), 1487-1506. He was a patron of historians and poets.

The Mughals were a Persian people who invaded northern India in the early 16th century. At its height the Mughal Empire embraced most of the Indian sub-continent. Akbar the Great (reigned 1556-1605) was followed by his son, Jahangir, and grandson, Shah Jahan, who built the Taj Mahal, 1632-47. From the mid 18th century, the power of the Mughal Emperors diminished as that of the British East India Company increased.

Trophy head, Asante treasure, 19th century or earlier (weighs 0.17kg) [OA1683]

The trophy head is part of the fabulous golden treasure of King Kofi Kakari of Asante, an ancient kingdom in Ghana, West Africa. The treasure was seized by British soldiers on the orders of their commander, Field-Marshal Viscount Wolseley, during the Asante campaign of 1873.

Most of the Asante treasure was taken from Coomassie, the gold-rich capital city of the Asante nation. The British government justified its decision to send an expeditionary force of soldiers to the Gold Coast of Africa by protesting that Asante warriors had been raiding settlements along the coast. It was an exceedingly hard-fought campaign and many lives were lost; it was also exceptionally unpopular with the British public.

Sir Richard Wallace bought the Asante treasure at a charitable auction in London, the proceeds of which were given to the wives and families of soldiers killed or incapacitated during the 1873 Asante War. It would appear that the motives for Wallace's acquisition were largely altruistic.

The sword belonged to Ranjit Singh, founder of the Sikh dynasty in the Punjab. The grip† is of ivory; the pommel† and quillons,† made from pure gold, terminate in bulls' heads. In the centre of the crossguard† is the figure of a tiger. The fine steel blade has an inherent rippling water effect enhanced by a chemical process ('watered steel').

The fine steel shield is decorated in gold with scenes of the hunt; warriors kill lions, antelope and hares with a variety of weapons. Its circumference bears the portraits and names of Sikh gurus. It is one of relatively few items of armour that can be specifically attributed to the Sikh kingdoms.

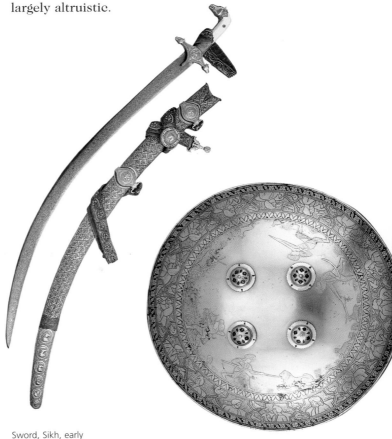

Sword, Sikh, early 19th century (92cm long) [OA1404]

Shield, Sikh, early 19th century (42 x 42cm) [OA2188]

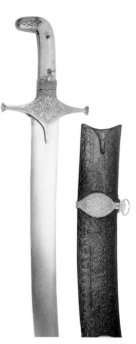

The hilt of the Indian straight-sword is decorated with a blue and white enamel horse's head complete with bridle. The details of nostrils, forelock, ears and eyes, picked out in gold, are exquisitely rendered.

The hilt of the rare Arabian shamshir† is mounted with gold. The base of the walrus-ivory grip is bound with a twisted gold wire.

Straight-sword, Indian, late 17th or 18th century (93.8cm long) [OA1432]

Shamshir, Arabian c.1800 (98.5cm long) [OA2002]

Horace Vernet *The Arab Tale-Teller* French 1833 (99 x 136.5cm)

Vernet painted *The Arab Tale-Teller* after his first visit to Algeria in 1833. A group of men sit in the shade of a fig tree, escaping the midday sun. They smoke and listen to a story told by the man in a grey and white striped robe, who sits on an oriental carpet. In the background are the tents, horses and livestock of the nomads. A girl resembling a classical statue stands with an urn on her shoulder while another, in the tent on the right, prepares wool for spinning.

In the 19th century, European artists admired north African and middle eastern peoples and cities because they were untouched by modern industrial development. They perceived a nobility in the native people and were inspired by scenes which they regarded as unchanged since the time of Christ.

Alexandre-Gabriel Decamps *The Turkish Patrol* French 1831 (114.5 x 179cm)

In *The Turkish Patrol*, nine foot-patrolmen accompany the mounted chief of police on his evening round of Smyrna (now Izmir in Turkey), which Decamps visited in 1828. A sense of speed and drama is effected by the acute angles of the figures, reminiscent of the sweeping curves and glittering sharp edges of oriental weapons. The chief carries a Turkish yataghan (short sword) in its scabbard and an Ottoman mace is visible across the horse's neck. Weapons carried by the patrol include a variety of eastern Mediterranean flint-lock long-guns and pistols. The man in the lead carries a European 17th-century wheel-lock pistol, which might have been traded or looted.

Helmet, Chinese, mid 19th century
(84cm high) [OA1701]

The superb helmet is part of the ceremonial court dress of a Chinese military mandarin. The skull of the helmet is silver mounted with pierced and gilt copper wings. On the front, four dragons protect the sacred sun jewels, a matrix of rubies. The crest of the helmet, covered with sable fur, is hung with a bunch of black human hair dyed red.

Kris dagger, Java, late 17th century
(42cm long in scabbard) [OA1630]

The kris[†] dagger has a carved ivory hilt and a scabbard overlaid with gold. The tip of the scabbard is set with rubies. The shape of the blade, which widens abruptly at the hilt, is characteristic of a kris.

Mandarins were important public officials in China. Different grades of military and civilian mandarins were entitled to wear different insignia on their costumes.

T he arms and armour in the European Armoury I, dating from the 10th to the early 16th centuries, were used for battle, for the tournament and for hunting. Richard Wallace acquired the European Armoury in 1871 when he bought the collections of the comte de Nieuwerkerke and Sir Samuel Rush Meyrick, the pioneer of the study of arms and armour in England.

The comte de Nieuwerkerke, Napoleon III's Minister of Fine Arts and Director of the Louvre, was a keen collector of arms, armour and medieval antiquities. Having fled France, he sold the majority of his collection to Richard Wallace in 1871. Other objects from Nieuwerkerke's collection are on display in the Sixteenth-Century Gallery and the Smoking Room.

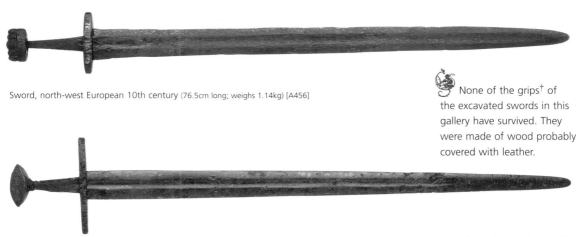

Sword, north-west European 10th century (76.5cm long; weighs 1.14kg) [A456]

None of the grips[†] of the excavated swords in this gallery have survived. They were made of wood probably covered with leather.

Sword, German 11th-12th century (82.2cm long; weighs 1.2kg) [A457]

Any Viking or Saxon warrior would have been proud to own the 10th-century sword. The crossguard[†] is overlaid with a silver alloy and decorated with a pattern and letters, possibly spelling the name of the swordsmith. The sword has a broad, double-edged blade designed principally for cutting and slashing.

The German sword is a fine example of a type of weapon used by European knights during the Crusades. Its pommel[†] is shaped like a brazil nut. The acutely pointed blade is suitable for cut and thrust action, reflecting the development in sword design caused by a demand for swords which could penetrate armour.

The Crusades, authorised by the Pope, were fought against enemies, chiefly Muslims, of the Western Christian Church. Crusaders sewed crosses on their clothes and were granted privileges by the Church. The First Crusade, 1096-9, captured the holy city of Jerusalem. The Second, 1145-9, was less successful. The Third Crusade, 1189-92, was dominated by Richard the Lionheart of England. Further crusades took place from the 13th to early 16th centuries.

Mail shirt, German 1425-50, detail (diameter of links: 1.03cm; weighs 8.84kg) [A2]

The mail shirt has a brass link at the neck signed with the name of its German maker, Bernart Couwein. Hand-forged riveted mail armour was probably invented by the Celts, perhaps as early as the 4th century BC. It was soon adopted by the Romans, and subsequently used by Saxons, Vikings, Normans and the Crusaders.

Mail was made by flattening the ends of an open circle of iron wire ('link'), interlinking it with another link, piercing the flattened ends with a hole and joining them with a tiny iron rivet. There might be 40,000 links in one mail shirt.

Sword, French 14th century
(76.2cm long; weighs 1.36kg) [A460]

Sword, French or Italian c.1460
(88.3cm long; weighs 1.34kg) [A466]

The French sword is an archetypal knight's sword from the era of the Hundred Years War. A wheel pommel has replaced the brazil nut shape and the quillons[†] are curved. The corrosion pattern on the blade was caused by the river in which the sword was found.

The gilt-bronze[†] hilt[†] of the sword dated c.1460 has a sculptural fish tail pommel. It is typical of swords found on the site of the battle of Castillon, the final defeat of the English in the Hundred Years War during which the English commander, John Talbot, was killed. When captured by the French in an earlier battle, he had vowed that he would never wear armour in battle against the French again. He kept his word and suffered so many wounds at Castillon that his dead body was barely recognisable.

During the Hundred Years War, 1337-1453, the French and English kings fought over territories in France. Famous battles were the defeat of the French at Crécy on 26 August 1346 and the battle of Agincourt on 25 October 1415, when Henry V led the English to victory. Joan of Arc saved Orléans from the English but was later captured and burned at Rouen on 30 May 1431. The Hundred Years War terminated with the defeat of the English at Castillon on 17 July 1453 and the loss of all territories previously won by Henry V.

Visored basinet, Italian c.1390
(26 x 37.4cm; weighs 4.07kg) [A69]

The rare basinet helmet was made in Milan. It would have been worn in battle and is of a type familiar in Europe throughout the Hundred Years War. The slits are for looking and breathing; the round holes, or 'breaths', are for breathing but also increase the field of vision. The steel helmet presents a smooth glancing surface in order to deflect blows struck from any angle. Its sophisticated design makes it very strong and yet relatively lightweight, an essential feature of any field armour (general purpose armour used primarily for war).

Initial 'A' with Galeazzo Maria Sforza in prayer (illuminated manuscript cutting), Italian c.1477, detail (in the Sixteenth-Century Gallery)

A full suit of armour was too expensive for the common soldier. A modern item of similar value would be a light aircraft or a Ferrari sports car. The armoured knight was able to move easily and dismount and mount his horse in the thick of battle. Forget the myth that he was winched on to his horse with a crane or that if he fell over he was not able to get up again. An average 15th or 16th-century field armour weighs 18 or 20 kg, less than half the weight of weaponry and kit carried into battle by a modern marine commando.

Falchion, Italian 1546-9
(61cm long; weighs 1.68kg) [A710]

Hunting was a favourite aristocratic pastime. The hunting field was a good testing ground for the strength, courage and endurance necessary to the warrior and it was the ideal place to show off the family weapons and to entertain friends and influential allies.

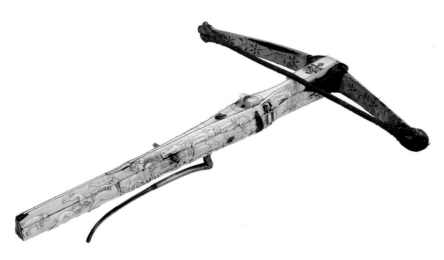

Crossbow, German, late 15th century
(span of bow: 23.5cm; weighs 4.4kg) [A1032]

The ornate falchion[†] was made for Cosimo de' Medici[†] for hunting and ceremonial use. The hilt, made from gilt steel, has quillons which end in lions' heads and a lion's head pommel. It is decorated with vine leaves and bunches of grapes chiselled in relief.

The magnificent crossbow, made in Bavaria, belonged to the Völs Colonna family from the Tyrol. The tiller (handle) is decorated with staghorn carved in relief with various scenes including a stag hunt, St George killing the dragon, Adam and Eve and the martyrdom of St Sebastian. The steel bow is covered with painted and gilded parchment. This crossbow was much too fine for battle; it was used for hunting.

Serving knife, French 1430-5 (41.1cm long) [A881]

The serving knife was made for Philip the Fair, Duke of Burgundy (1396-1467), and bears his arms and motto. The haft (handle) is made from silver-gilt[†] inlaid with coloured enamels. A serving knife as grand as this would have been used for the ceremonial presentation of food at the table.

In the 14th and 15th centuries, the duchy of Burgundy acquired territorial power which rivalled even the kingdom of France. It included French Burgundy, Holland, Belgium and parts of Northern France and Germany. The Burgundian court was one of the most magnificent in Europe.

Great helm, English or Flemish c.1420
(34.6cm high; weighs 7.4kg) [A186]

The great helm was made
for jousting. It fastened
front and back to the jouster's
body-armour and was much
less flexible than field armour.
The jouster saw and breathed
through the helmet's frog-mouth.
Inflexibility and narrow vision
were not important as the
jouster was concerned solely
with protecting himself from
a single opponent attacking
from the front.

Most armour was hammered
into shape out of red-hot
iron or steel. Iron was used
until improvements in
technology gradually
replaced it with steel. By
the 14th and 15th centuries,
much aristocratic armour
was made of steel.

Tournament shield, German c.1480-5 (53.7cm high; weighs 4.62kg) [A309]

The tournament shield was intended for the 'Renneug', a form of
joust fashionable at the Imperial Court of the Holy Roman Empire
in Germany. The large cut-out accommodated the jouster's lance.
The shield is made of wood covered with leather and painted
with a gilt foliage pattern and an inscription on a scroll.

Tournaments usually
had three phases: jousting
with a lance against a mounted
opponent, combat on foot and
the melée, in which a group
of knights, usually mounted,
fought another group. By the
15th century, many individual
combats were fought 'at the
barriers', the contestants
separated by a stout wooden
fence. Mounted combat was
made safer by separating the
opponents with a tilt barrier,
thus avoiding the danger of
collision. 'Jousting' is any
mounted lance combat.
'Tilting' is jousting with a tilt
barrier. Jousts were carefully
controlled and hitting 'below
the belt' was strictly forbidden.

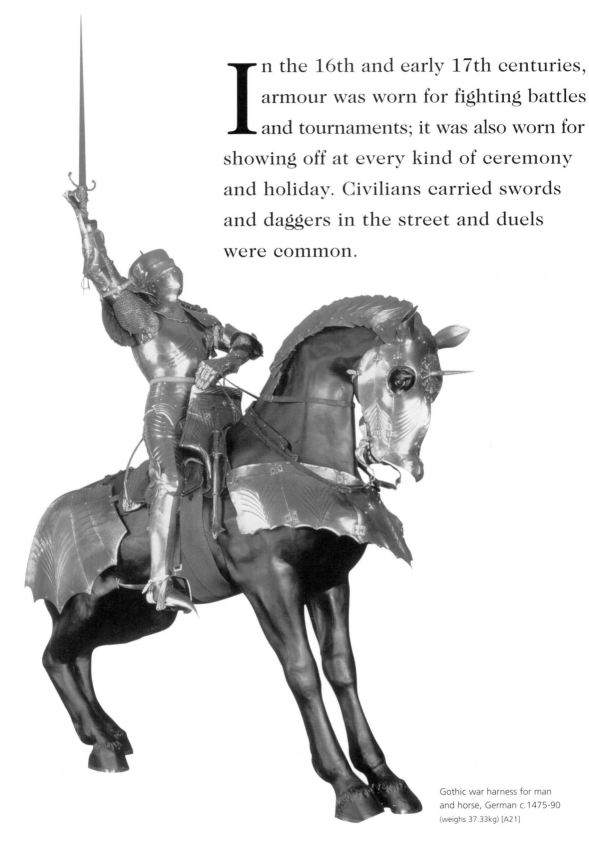

In the 16th and early 17th centuries, armour was worn for fighting battles and tournaments; it was also worn for showing off at every kind of ceremony and holiday. Civilians carried swords and daggers in the street and duels were common.

Gothic war harness for man
and horse, German c.1475-90
(weighs 37.33kg) [A21]

The famous equestrian armour came from the Von Freyberg family castle in the Tyrol. Although partly composite with a number of 19th-century restorations, the armour is historically very important. The horse armour is largely genuine and extremely rare. The shaffron (armour for a horse's head) bears the city mark of Landshut, and a master-mark 'R' which is ascribed to Ulrich Rämbs. Other parts of the armour were probably also made in Landshut.

Close helmet for the tournament, German 1555
(weighs 5.62kg) [A188]

The close helmet is perhaps the
finest and most valuable helmet
in the armoury. It was made
in 1555 by Conrad Richter of
Augsburg as part of the famous
Golden Garniture ordered by
the future Holy Roman Emperor,
Ferdinand I, for himself and his
three sons. The entire surface
was covered in acid-etched
decoration and then mercury-
gilded.[†] Ferdinand I was the son
of Charles V (reigned 1519-58)
and grandson of Maximilian I
(reigned 1493-1519).

The garniture was developed in the latter part of the 15th century. Purpose-made
interchangeable elements could be 'mixed and matched' to alter an armour for
different pursuits such as war, parade or tournament. In the 16th century, larger
garnitures ran to hundreds of individual pieces.

The Holy Roman Empire,
which existed until 1806,
derived from the Christian
Empire of Charlemagne. It
included Germany and northern
Italy. All Emperors were elected
by the seven German princes of
Brandenburg, Saxony, Bohemia,
Mainz, Treves, Cologne and the
Palatinate, who were known
as Electors.

Cannon, Venetian 1688 (139cm long) [A1245]

The bronze barrel of the cannon
is intricately cast with scenes of
Hercules battling with the Titans.
The barrel was made in Venice –
there is a legend that it was found
in the Venetian lagoon – and the
carriage was built in 1853-4 for
Prince Anatole Demidoff of San
Donato in Florence. He displayed
the cannon, which was made for
show rather than war, as a centre-
piece in his palace Armoury.

The armour of Lord Buckhurst, later 1st Earl of Dorset, reflects late-Tudor fashion. It was made in the Royal workshops in Greenwich, established by Henry VIII at the beginning of the 16th century. The form and profile of the armour mirror an Elizabethan gentleman's fashionable civilian attire: a pronounced peascod doublet, with a point at the waist, and an extravagantly puffed trunk-hose (over-hose reaching from waist to middle thigh).

This is the only English suit of armour in the armoury. The steel plates are etched and mercury-gilded. The plain areas originally would have been a deep bright blue, achieved by heating the steel to a temperature of 350°C. Despite its rich appearance, this armour was made for war. Lord Buckhurst probably ordered it in anticipation of the imminent arrival of the Spanish Armada (1588). The armour is a small garniture: it was supplied with extra pieces which could be attached to the outside of existing pieces for reinforcement.

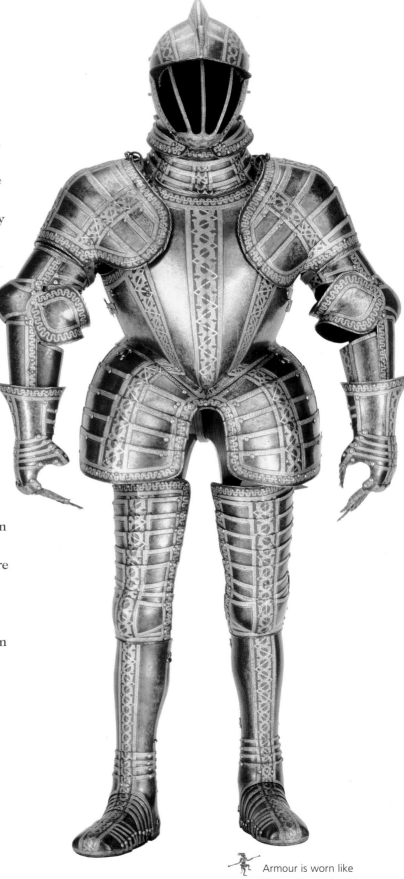

Lord Buckhurst's armour, English c.1587
(weighs 32.02kg) [A62]

Armour is worn like clothing and so it should be no surprise that its form and design followed that of fashionable dress.

Parade shield, Italian c.1560
(67.3 x 55.1cm; weighs 4.11kg) [A325]

The parade shield, made in Milan, is of superlative quality. It is embossed, silvered and gilded with a scene representing the surrender of Carthage to the Romans. It bears the cypher of King Henri II of France and was perhaps made to celebrate the surrender of Calais by the English in 1558.

Those who could afford it wore richly decorated parade armour at ceremonies, feasts and holidays. It was not worn for fighting but simply to show off. By the end of the 16th century, the Italians had achieved a considerable reputation as manufacturers of parade armour, often supplied with horse armour and other accessories to match.

Henri IV's left-hand dagger was given to him with a companion rapier[†] (now in the Musée de l'Armée, Paris) by the city of Paris on the occasion of his marriage to Maria de' Medici. (Henri IV, King of France, married Maria de' Medici by proxy in Florence.) The rapier was carried by Napoleon Bonaparte on campaign throughout Europe as a 'good-luck' mascot.

The swept-hilt rapier, made for a wealthy gentleman, is silver encrusted with gilt decoration. It was dug up in Saffron Walden, Essex, in the 19th century.

The 16th century was the era of rapier-and-dagger duelling. The dagger was held in the left hand and the rapier in the right. Duels ranged from street brawls – Tybalt was killed with a rapier in Shakespeare's *Romeo and Juliet* – to engagements governed by formal rules and fought in the name of honour between gentlemen.

Henri IV's left-hand dagger, French c.1600
(blade: 24cm long; weighs 0.27kg) [A790]

Swept-hilt rapier,
English c.1605-15
(113.4cm long; weighs
1.29kg) [A596]

The arms and armour in the European Armoury III range from the 16th to the 19th centuries. In this period the fully-armoured knight was driven from the battlefield by the rise of firearms. The array of sporting guns, rifles and pistols, including magnificent flint-locks of the Napoleonic era, constitutes the finest collection of firearms in the country.

Armour for man and horse, German 1532-6 (weighs 54.87kg) [A29]

The equestrian armour was made in Nuremberg for the middle-aged Count Otto Heinrich, Elector Palatine. Armour, like clothing, was made to fit the wearer and you can tell from the shape of this armour that the Count was much older and fatter than Count von Freyburg, who wore the equestrian armour displayed in European Armoury II. The change in style, for example the broad, blunt toes of the sabatons (armour over-shoes), reflects the change in dress fashion after thirty or more years. The armour is painted black, etched and gilded. The breastplate is decorated with the Virgin and Child on a crescent moon.

Cuirassier (heavy cavalry) armour was worn by some troops in the English Civil War. Firearms were becoming more effective on the battlefield and cuirassier armour was designed to be shot-proof – you can see the dent in the breastplate made by the 'proving' bullet fired by the armourer. Bullet-proof armour had to be extra thick, making it very heavy. It soon became clear that full suits of armour were more of an encumbrance than an aid to survival. The standard cavalry equipment became breastplate and helmet, which remained popular well into the 19th century.

Cuirassier armour, German c.1630
(weighs 20.25kg) [A65]

Sword breaker, Italian c.1600
(50.8cm long; weighs 0.81kg) [A868]

Oliver Cromwell defeated King Charles I's royalist army in the English Civil War, 1642-6. Famous battles were fought at Edgehill, Marston Moor and Naseby. The King's Oxford headquarters surrendered in 1646 and, on 30 January 1649, the King was executed and a Commonwealth declared.

The sword breaker was designed to disarm an opponent, trapping or breaking his sword blade in the barbed teeth.

How did you put your armour on? Armour had to be very comfortable. It was worn over an arming doublet – a padded jacket sewn with straps and laces to which individual pieces of armour were secured. This helped to distribute the weight over the body. Vulnerable areas, for example the neck, the groin and the armpits, were given extra protection by sewing patches of mail to the arming doublet.

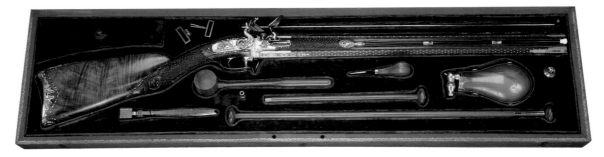

Double-barrelled flint-lock rifle, French c.1805 (102cm long; weighs 3.61kg) [A1126]

The rare double-barrelled flint-lock rifle is complete with the tools necessary to clean and load it. It was probably ordered by the Emperor Napoleon and was made by Nicolas-Noël Boutet, the most famous gun-maker in Europe, in his factory at Versailles. It was subsequently owned by Tsar Nicholas I of Russia, whose gilt cypher appears on the case lid. Cased sets of this quality are very rare.

A wheel-lock is an ignition mechanism, developed in the early 16th century. Gunpowder is ignited by sparks produced by stone (iron pyrite) rubbing against a revolving serrated steel wheel. Flint-locks were developed in the early 17th century. Sparks are produced by a piece of flint striking steel.

Wheel-lock sporting gun, German c.1620 (170cm long; weighs 5.25kg) [A1090]

The wheel-lock sporting gun was made for a member of the Bavarian Electoral Court in Munich by the celebrated Sadeler family of metalworkers and iron-chisellers and the gunstock master, Hieronymous Borstorffer. Their craftsmanship was supreme. The stock and barrel are gilded and chiselled in low relief with classical figures including Bacchus, god of wine, and Diana, goddess of hunting. This gun was part of the impressive personal collection of Napoleon III of France.

Blunderbuss, Russian 1780
(91cm long; weighs 2.79kg) [A1124]

The superb silver-mounted blunderbuss[†] was made by Johan Grecke, the Court gun-maker in St Petersburg. It bears the cypher of the Empress Catherine II of Russia.

First Floor

The Landing is rich with the symbolism of the French Sun King. It is hung with pairs of mythological and theatrical paintings by Boucher.

Staircase balustrade, French 1719-20

The staircase balustrade is made from cast and wrought iron and gilt brass.[†] A heart-shaped cartouche frames the interlaced 'L's of Louis XV. If you trace the S and C-shaped scrolls you will find sunflowers, a reference to the Sun King. Horns of plenty overflow with fruit, coins and banknotes, a reference to the wealth promised by France's new banking system.

The balustrade was commissioned for a building in Paris which in 1719 was destined to become the Royal Bank. However, a year later the entire financial system crashed and five years after that the building became the King's Library. Bought by Richard Wallace, the balustrade was altered to fit Hertford House and installed in 1874.

Staircase balustrade, detail

One of the coins bears a bust of the youthful Louis XV.

Hertford House, 1790-97

Hertford House was built in 1776-78 for the 4th Duke of Manchester who was attracted by the good duck shooting in the area. It comprised five bays and a Venetian window. After a brief spell as the Spanish Embassy, it was bought by the 2nd Marquess of Hertford in 1797. He added the conservatory, in place of the Venetian window, on the Landing and two first-floor rooms on each wing.

François Boucher *A Summer Pastoral*
French 1749 (259 x 197cm)

François Boucher *An Autumn Pastoral*
French 1749 (259 x 197cm)

A Summer Pastoral and *An Autumn Pastoral* depict characters from Favart's pantomimes, which combine the sensibilities of pastoral poetry with the rustic characters of popular theatre. *Summer* shows the cousins Babette and Lisette with the Little Shepherd. He serenades his sweetheart, Lisette, on the *musette* (bagpipes) to win the crown of flowers held at her side. *Autumn* depicts a scene from a pantomime first performed in 1745: the Little Shepherd feeds grapes to the heroine, Lisette. Boucher designed theatre sets for his friend, Favart.

Filippo della Valle *Cupid and Psyche*
Italian c.1732 (83.8cm high)

The representation of the mythological lovers Psyche[†] and Cupid as children of the same age, rather than adults, is an unusual treatment of the subject. The soft modelling of the features, the pliant limbs and dimples in soft childish flesh contribute to a provocative meeting of innocence and desire.

François Boucher *The Rising of the Sun* French 1753 (318 x 261cm)

The Rising and *The Setting* incurred fierce criticism at the 1753 Salon.[†] One commentator complained that their excessive nudity was so shocking that one should not take one's wife or daughter to the Salon.

Every day Apollo, the sun god, rises from the river Oceanus, which surrounds the earth, and drives his chariot across the heavens bringing light to the world. In the evening he sinks back beneath the waves where he is attended by the nymph, Tethys, and the sons and daughters of the sea. In *The Rising*, Apollo prepares for his journey across the sky while Tethys holds the reins of his white horses. Meanwhile Aurora, goddess of the dawn, sets out to scatter her pink roses across the sky. She is crowned by the Morning Star and behind her winged infants push back the clouds of night. In *The Setting*, Apollo has completed his journey and dismounts from his chariot into the open arms of Tethys. Far above him shines the Evening Star and winged infants pull across the dark clouds of night.

Madame de Pompadour, Louis XV's mistress, ordered tapestries based on Boucher's paintings and both paintings and tapestries at one time hung in her château at Bellevue. The scenes derive from Ovid's *Metamorphoses*.[†] Madame de Pompadour was clearly involved in the choice of iconography for the paintings, indulging in shameless self-aggrandisement by casting herself in the role of Tethys welcoming home Louis XV after a hard day with affairs of state.

François Boucher *The Setting of the Sun* French 1752 (318 x 261cm)

Bomb damage at Hertford House
September 1940

Evacuation of the collection
August 1939

*H*ertford House narrowly escaped destruction in the Blitz of World War II.
In the courtyard floor you can see a paving stone which flew over the roof
in 1940. Fortunately the collection had already been evacuated.

The Small Drawing Room is hung with the 18th-century Grand Tourist's equivalent of modern holiday snaps and souvenirs. Imagine the Grand Tourist's satisfaction when he saw his purchases hanging on the walls of his ancestral home on his return from a two year tour of France and Italy.

Canaletto *Venice: the Bacino di San Marco from the Canale della Giudecca*
Italian c.1735-44 (130.2 x 190.8cm)

The pair of unusually large views by Canaletto look across the Bacino di San Marco from opposite directions. *The Bacino from the Canale della Giudecca* shows the view from the mouth of the Giudecca Canal looking across the Bacino towards the church of San Giorgio. On the left is the Dogana (Customs House) surmounted by a golden globe with a figure of Fortune.

Between 1725 and 1740, Canaletto specialised almost exclusively in views of Venice. They were much sought after by English Grand Tourists who wished to take home a souvenir of the cosmopolitan city where West met East.

A The Canalettos were bought
by the 1st Marquess who was
himself a Grand Tourist.
He travelled in France and
Italy in 1738 and 1739.

The Grand Tour flourished throughout the 18th century. It was
interrupted by the French Revolution and by the Napoleonic Wars, but
after 1815 travellers again flocked to Italy. Young men made the Tour to
complete their education, to admire the remains of the classical past and
to collect art and antiquities. (One British nobleman brought home 878
pieces of luggage from his 1719 tour.) The journey was usually made
through France and Italy. Paris was essential; the Italian tour embraced
Florence, Naples and Venice and the climax was a lengthy period in Rome.

Canaletto *Venice: the Bacino di San Marco from San Giorgio Maggiore*
Italian c.1735-44 (130.2 x 190.8cm)

Canaletto adapted his style to suit his patrons: he produced clearly
identifiable views with picturesque figures in local costume. They
were painted in bright colours on relatively small canvases which
were easy to transport.

The Bacino from San Giorgio Maggiore shows the view from the
steps of the church of San Giorgio looking across the Bacino towards
the mouth of the Giudecca Canal. In the foreground different levels of
Venetian society are depicted: a beggar sits on the right; oriental
merchants discuss business in the centre; a lawyer and priests
converse on the left. In the middle ground a passenger barge is
towed by a boat with four oarsmen. Covered gondolas sweep past
ships at anchor. The ships fly the Dutch, British and Venetian flags.

Chinese lacquer starts life as the sap of the *rhus vernicifera* tree, a grey syrupy juice which becomes plastic on exposure to air. It is applied to a material such as wood in numerous very thin layers, each of which must dry before the next coat is added. Here the lacquer is dyed black and decorated with gilding and coloured lacquer.

Marchand, Commode (chest of drawers)
French 1755 (84.5 x 86.5 x 55.8cm)

The commode is one of a pair delivered to the French royal palace of Fontainebleau for the bedroom of Queen Marie Leczinska, wife of Louis XV. It is veneered with panels of Chinese lacquer in a way which ignores the logic of the pictorial decoration on the lacquer, a common occurrence in French 18th-century furniture making. Notice how the gilt-bronze[†] mounts incorporate drawer handles.

Charles Cressent, Cartel clock
French c.1747 (135.9 x 52.7 x 35.6cm)

The gilt-bronze case of the cartel clock represents Love triumphing over Time. Love, who has insect wings, sits on a bank of cloud on top of the clock. Beside him is a winged hour-glass which he has stolen from Time. Underneath the dial the defeated figure of Time wields his scythe. The superb case of the cartel clock, which is designed to hang on the wall, is more like sculpture than furniture. Cressent, a cabinet maker, was prosecuted by both the bronze founders and the gilders on metal for having bronzes cast and gilded on his premises, contrary to guild regulations.

Love triumphing over Time was a favourite subject with French clockmakers. The allegory was first used by André-Charles Boulle c.1695. He based his figures on a renaissance woodcut. Time's attributes are a scythe, with which he reaps lives, and scales, used for weighing good and evil on the dreadful day of judgement. In Boulle's models, Love flies away with Time's scythe.

The Large Drawing Room and the adjoining Oval Drawing Room were ballrooms in the time of the 2nd Marquess. His wife was famous for the sumptuous dinners, receptions and balls which she gave.

In 1814 the Marchioness held a ball to celebrate the defeat of Napoleon, who was in exile in Elba. The guests of honour were the Prince Regent and Britain's allies, the Emperor of Russia and the King of Prussia. The floor of the ballroom was painted with allegories of Peace and Plenty and the Russian spread-eagle. A sumptuous banquet was laid out in the ground floor rooms. A newspaper reported, 'the Imperial hero was the first to lead the gayest of the throng with waltzes, in every one of which the Emperor gave the true German *fling* to the great delight of the company.' The party ended at five o'clock in the morning.

Benjamin Franklin was sent to Paris in 1776 to persuade Louis XVI to recognise American independence from Britain. He had to wait over a year and was beloved by Court ladies and Parisian intellectuals alike. The King ratified American independence in 1777. The Sèvres factory produced busts and portrait medallions of Franklin which were copied throughout Europe.

Cup and saucer
French c.1788-80 (7.6 x 14.8cm)

Vase and cover, French 1768 (54.4 x 21.5cm)

The remarkable vase, which was displayed in the Large Drawing Room in the Wallaces' day, and the cup and saucer are made of Sèvres porcelain.† The vase's column-like shape and the Greek-key pattern around the rim are in the neo-classical style. Extraordinary zig-zag handles descend like folded pastry. The vase would have appeared startlingly *avant garde* in 1768.

The cup has a portrait of Benjamin Franklin and the saucer is painted with an American-Indian head-dress and a bow and arrow lying on a shield bearing *fleurs de lis* (the French royal emblem), to mark the Franco-American alliance of 1778.

Neo-classicism, which superseded the rococo, began to emerge in France in the 1750s. The new taste was shaped and stimulated by recent excavations at Herculaneum and Pompeii. It is characterised by the use of Greek and Roman architectural ornament, by a preference for sober colours and by linear, rather than richly sculptural, decoration.

Francesco Guardi
Venice: the Dogana with the Giudecca
Venice: San Giorgio Maggiore with the Giudecca and the Zitelle
Italian 1770-6 (68 x 90cm)

Francesco Guardi
Venice: the Grand Canal with the Riva del Vin and the Rialto Bridge
Venice: Santa Maria della Salute and the Dogana
Italian 1770-6 (68 x 90cm)

The topographical views by Guardi are the only set of four which are still together today. They are typical of the limpid, atmospheric views for which he is famous. *The Dogana with the Giudecca* looks across the mouth of the Grand Canal to the Dogana (customs house) and the island of the Guidecca. *The Grand Canal with the Riva del Vin and the Rialto Bridge* shows the Rialto Bridge with the Riva del Vin shoreline on the left and the Fondaco dei Tedeschi (German foundry) visible beyond the bridge on the right.

San Giorgio Maggiore with the Giudecca and the Zitelle looks across the Bacino towards the church of San Giorgio and the Benedictine monastery. The island of the Giudecca and the dome of the Zitelle church are in the distance on the right. *Santa Maria della Salute and the Dogana* shows a view from the Grand Canal towards the Dogana with the church of Santa Maria della Salute on the right.

Guardi's early views were clearly influenced by Canaletto. After 1770 his style developed: his brushwork became looser, his colours lighter and topography took second place to atmospheric effect. Effervescent figures are brushed on to the canvas with a few bravura strokes.

Claude-Joseph Vernet *A Storm with a Shipwreck*
French 1754 (87 x 137cm)

A Storm with a Shipwreck,
commissioned by Madame
de Pompadour's brother, was
painted by Vernet whilst living
in Marseilles. A beleaguered ship
is dashed against the rocks
while a rescue boat, on the left,
struggles against the odds. A
half-drowned woman swoons
on a rocky outcrop on the
right. Meanwhile, fascinated
onlookers make their way
down from the castle to
watch the awful spectacle.

Mantel clock, French *c.*1715 (79 x 53.5 x 42cm)

The case of the mantel clock
is attributed to André-Charles
Boulle. The beautiful dial is
cast in low relief with six flying
infants who each support an
hour number.

The chimney piece in the Oval Drawing Room is dated c.1785 and is the only one to survive *in situ*. Hertford House, originally called 'Manchester House', was built for the 4th Duke of Manchester between 1776 and 1778.

Mantel clock, French c.1775 (68 x 100.7 x 25cm)

The mantel clock is a neo-classical version of a model by André-Charles Boulle created in the early years of the 18th century. The bronze figures of Night and Day, which recline against the dial, are based on figures by Michelangelo. The female figure of Night sleeps with her left arm resting on a bearded mask. An owl perches in the hollow of her leg.

In 1816 Captain Gronow had recently returned from Paris where 'knee-breeches were worn only by a few old fogies.' He went to a party at Hertford House dressed in black trousers '*à la française.*' He found the Prince Regent 'in the octagon room [Oval Drawing Room], surrounded by all the great ladies of the Court,' and made his bow. Gronow wrote, 'I sat down by the beautiful Lady Hertford, and had been engaged in conversation with her for some time, when Horace Seymour tapped me on the shoulder and said "The Great Man," meaning the Prince, "is very much surprised that you should have ventured to appear in his presence without knee-breeches."'

The gilt-bronze[†] wall-light is one of a pair. The candle branches end in eagles' heads which look in different directions. Below the satyr's mask, cymbals and Pan-pipes are suspended on ribbons with simulated tassels at the ends. The wall lights were probably supplied either for the bedroom of Madame Adélaïde (daughter of Louis XV) or for Marie-Antoinette's bedroom.

Wall light, French c.1780 (93.5 x 39 x 28.7

Martin Carlin, Reading and writing table
French 1783-4 (79 x 40.7 x 32.8cm)

Jean-Baptiste Boulard, Chair
French 1786 (93.4 x 57.4 x 50.6cm)

The table is veneered with tulipwood[†] and mounted with plaques of Sèvres porcelain.[†] Behind the drop-front are two drawers, one of which is fitted for writing materials. The table-top is raised on vertical steel racks and writing slides and candle-stands pull out from the sides. The porcelain plaque on top tilts up to serve as a book-rest. The whole top is revolved by pressing a knob at the back. The table was made for the *marchand-mercier* Daguerre.

The chair is one of a set made for Louis XVI's card room at the royal palace of Fontainebleau. Chairs with separate cushions were intended for ladies. It is covered with blue patterned silk, an exact reproduction of its original covering.

Marchand-merciers were dealers in furniture and works of art. They exercised great influence over taste by controlling the designers and craftsmen they employed. The fashion for decorating furniture with Sèvres plaques was almost certainly due to the *marchand-merciers*. Daguerre was one of the most famous.

Elizabeth-Louise Vigée Le Brun *Madame Perregaux* French 1789 (98.5 x 77cm)

Vigée Le Brun (1755-1842) had beauty and style which aided her professional success. She first painted Marie-Antoinette in 1778. It was partly due to the Queen that she was received by the French Royal Academy in 1783. She left Paris in 1789, escaping the French Revolution. She visited London and stayed briefly in Portman Square, next to Manchester Square where the 2nd Marquess was residing in Hertford House.

The French Royal Academy of Painting and Sculpture was founded under Louis XIV. It was distinguished from the Guild by its teaching, which had an intellectual as opposed to a purely manual content. The emphasis was on design rather than making and the Academy raised the status of painters from craftsmen to artists. Academy members' work was exhibited at annual or biennial Salons and prizes were awarded. History painting was regarded as pre-eminent because it was perceived to have the greatest intellectual content.

Madame Perregaux is a portrait of the wife of a banker, J.-F. Perregaux (the 3rd Marquess was his client). Vigée Le Brun had a particular approach to her female subjects: 'I try as much as I can to give the women I paint the attitude and expression of their physiognomy...' She selected a pose for the sitter 'suitable to her age and character, which can add to the resemblance.'

Greuze exhibited *Votive offering to Cupid* at the 1769 Salon. He had been successful as a genre[†] painter but his ambition was to be accepted as a history painter. The Academy rejected him. Diderot[†] wrote 'Greuze knows the *beau idéal* in his own genre but not here.'

Jean-Baptiste Greuze *Votive offering to a Cupid* French 1765-9 (145.5 x 113cm)

Jean-Henri Riesener, Roll-top desk
French c.1770 (139 x 195.5 x 102.5cm)

The top of the desk rolls back to reveal drawers, sliding trays and a writing surface fitted with velvet-lined panels. The desk is veneered with pictorial marquetry of holly, walnut, ebony,[†] box and sycamore. On the top, letters in French and German lie amongst notebooks, one with an elaborately marbled cover; also a seal with the arms of the comte d'Orsay (the desk was supplied for the Hôtel d'Orsay in Paris), quill pens, a stick of sealing wax, a pen-knife, an inkwell, a sand box and three sponges. A personification of Silence, a young woman holding her finger to her lips, is on the back of the desk. On her left is a terrestrial globe with the attributes of geometry, including a protractor and a half-rolled map. On the right is a celestial globe with the attributes of astronomy, including a half-rolled chart and a telescope.

Riesener (1734-1806) was the most successful cabinet maker of the Louis XVI period and perhaps the best of all French furniture makers. Born in Germany, Riesener joined Oeben's workshop in Paris. He became the manager on Oeben's death, ousting his rival, Leleu, and four years later, he married Oeben's widow. In 1774 he was appointed Cabinet Maker to Louis XVI. He survived the French Revolution and was employed by the new government to remove royal emblems from furniture.

Many pieces of French 18th-century furniture were fitted with secret compartments. Underneath the writing surface of the Riesener desk is a secret well with three small drawers at the back. The well is opened by releasing a catch at the side of the knee-hole recess.

Roll-top desk, detail

Jean-Marc Nattier *Mademoiselle de Clermont as a Sultana* French 1733 (109 x 104.5cm)

Mademoiselle de Clermont is painted as a Sultana taking a bath. Attention is focused on the handsome person of Mademoiselle whose bare legs are placed in the centre of the composition. She is attended by servants and eunuchs.

One dries her little foot; another gazes adoringly at her while fingering a string of pearls, a reminder of the pearl-white skin of his mistress. Rich textiles and a sumptuous Turkey carpet add to an atmosphere of lavish exoticism.

Turqueries depict figures in Turkish or oriental dress amidst oriental surroundings. They were the fashion in Paris in the 1720s and 30s, particularly after the visit of the Ottoman Ambassador, Méhémet-Effendi in 1721. Turkish subjects, with their sultans, harems and Turkish baths, licensed a certain wantonness and allowed those having their portraits painted to appear in a state of undress whilst maintaining their respectability.

Sir Richard Wallace answered his letters and dealt with his private affairs in his Study.

Sir Richard Wallace's Study, c. 1890

Queen Victoria created Richard Wallace a baronet in August 1871 in recognition of his work during the 1870-1 siege of Paris by the Prussians. During the winter, a British charitable fund was established to distribute relief. Wallace became its chairman and ran it most efficiently. He had just inherited a vast fortune from his father, the 4th Marquess, and he made a number of large charitable donations.

Napoleon III, Emperor of the French, declared war against Prussia in July 1870. On 2nd September, the Emperor surrendered at Sedan with 80,000 men. He was taken prisoner and the Prussian army began its advance on Paris.

Tray, French 1779 (48 x 37cm)

The tray is part of a tea service made of hard-paste Sèvres porcelain.† Guns blaze as a marine battle rages on the tray. The chinoiserie† scenes may have been inspired by drawings produced by Jesuit missionaries in China for the Emperor Ch'ien Lung, c.1760-75. Most Jesuits had been exiled from China but a few were allowed to remain at the Court in Peking. Earlier in the century they had enjoyed toleration and favour in return for scientific services.

In 18th-century France, tea, coffee and chocolate were taken in bedrooms, boudoirs, salons, gardens and in the bath. Tea was taken at breakfast and at formal receptions, for pleasure and for its medicinal properties.

Ice-cream cooler, French 1778 (23.7 x 26.2cm)

Catherine II became Empress of Russia in 1762 by overthrowing her husband, Tsar Peter III. She read the works of the Enlightenment, corresponded with Voltaire[†] and entertained Diderot.[†] She had twelve lovers, selecting younger and younger men as she grew older.

The ice-cream cooler was one of ten ice-cream coolers in a dinner service of 800 items ordered from the Sèvres factory by Empress Catherine II. The urn kept ice-creams or sorbets cool in a porcelain or tin liner. The cover, decorated with gilded icicles and a frozen fountain handle, was packed with ice for extra insulation.

Cup and saucer, French 1765 (8.3 x 15.3cm)

The cup and saucer, made of Sèvres porcelain, were used for tea, coffee or chocolate. The eye-catching decoration is bizarre for 1765.

Boulle workshop, Wardrobe
French c.1700 (255 x 163.5 x 61cm)

The imposing wardrobe is veneered with brass and tortoiseshell Boulle marquetry in a symmetrical design. Gilt-bronze[†] groups illustrate stories from Ovid's *Metamorphoses*.[†] On the left, Apollo, the sun god, pursues Daphne who is transformed into a laurel tree by her river-god father. On the right, Apollo orders the Scythian, who has a knife between his teeth, to flay Marsyas, who is bound to a tree. Apollo beat Marsyas in a musical contest, the winner of which was entitled to inflict his chosen penalty on the loser.

Lady Wallace's Boudoir was her private sitting-room. Miniatures and small paintings hung on the walls and Sèvres porcelain was exhibited under Victorian glass domes. Today it is hung with pictures by Greuze and Reynolds, painters who gave expression to the 18th-century cult of *sensibilité* in France and England.

The Boudoir, 1890s

Writing table (75.4 x 143.5 x 73cm)
Filing cabinet (214.1 x 73.1 x 41cm)
Inkstand (15.3 x 44.3 x 17cm)
French c.1765

An 18th-century gentleman might administer his affairs sitting at the writing table. Pens stood in the holes at the left of the boat-shaped inkstand, ink in the container with a solid lid and sand, to dry the ink, in the container with the pierced lid. Documents could be stored in leather-fronted boxes fitted to the three open compartments in the filing cabinet, or under lock and key in a cupboard in the base. All three pieces are lacquered with green French vernis.[†] On the top of the filing cabinet is a gilt-bronze[†] group of Cupid and Psyche.[†] Notice the flaming heart which Psyche holds in her right hand.

Joshua Reynolds *The Strawberry Girl*
English 1773 (76.1 x 63.1cm)

The Strawberry Girl is a 'fancy picture', a pleasing study of a figure, usually a child, in fancy dress. The subject of the picture, characteristic of the age of sensibility, is sentiment rather than narrative. This picture was regarded by Reynolds as one of his best works and he repeated the composition many times. The surface of the painting has darkened over time.

Rousseau (1712-1778), French philosopher, wrote that art must be liberated from the intellect if it is to give expression to human experience and allow 'heart to speak to heart.' *Sensibilité* is art's capacity to appeal to human sentiment. It also implies a person's capacity to be moved by art.

Jean-Baptiste Greuze
The Broken Mirror
French, before 1763 (56 x 45.6cm)

The Broken Mirror is a parable of carelessness. The disarray of the interior and the girl's dress reflect her dissolute morals. The shattered mirror symbolises the loss of her virginity. Her ringless hand and the yapping dog, a familiar symbol of carnal desire, draw our attention.

Greuze (1725-1805) was accepted by the French Royal Academy of Painting and Sculpture as a genre[†] painter. His moral scenes were praised by Diderot[†] as 'dramatic poetry to touch us, teach us, to correct us and incite us to virtue!' When the Academy rejected his history paintings, Greuze withdrew and exhibited privately in his studio. He achieved financial success with small-scale, expressive heads of young girls.

Jean-Baptiste Greuze *Innocence*
French 1790s (63 x 53cm)

A girl shows *sensibilité* in
embracing a lamb, symbol of
innocence, gentleness, patience
and humility. She is a heady
combination of youth, beauty,
sexual innocence and emotion.
In the 19th century, this was one
of the most famous paintings in
the world and made an appearance
in a *Sherlock Holmes* novel.

Richard Cosway *Maria Fagnani
('Mie-Mie'), 3rd Marchioness
of Hertford* 1791
(Wallace Collection Archives)

The 4th Marquess
delighted in pretty
pictures of tender young
women – 'with me fancy
plays a great part and
sometimes a very fine
picture does not please
me.' He consciously
avoided 'male'
subjects and had a
great enthusiasm for
Greuze's female heads.

The 4th Marquess
seemed incapable of
loving any woman
other than his mother,
Mie-Mie. It is said that
he always slept with
her miniature portrait
under his pillow. It
has a lock of her hair
set in the back.

Joshua Reynolds *Miss Jane Bowles*
English 1775 (91 x 70.9cm)

Miss Jane Bowles is a portrait
of a 3 or 4 year old girl. One
account tells how Reynolds
played tricks with Jane at table
so that later she sat for him
'with a face full of glee.' Reynolds
greatly admired Greuze, and this
painting displays a *sensibilité*
akin to Greuze's portraits of
small children with animals.

Jean Ducrollay, Snuff box
French 1743-4 (3.2 x 7.6 x 5.8cm)

Jean-Charles-Simphorien Dubos, Snuff box
French 1760-1 (3.9 x 8.6 x 6.7cm)

For an intimate view of the luxury world of 18th-century France, feast your eyes on 'the finest collection of French gold boxes in the world.' The shape, materials and decoration of these deliciously extravagant, personal toys were chosen to reflect the latest fashion.

The Ducrollay box is shaped like a scallop shell. It is enamelled to resemble a white peacock's fan-tail which, seen from the back, rises in full display as the cover is raised.

The Dubos box is made of four-colour gold – silver, copper and iron were added to colour the gold. The relief decoration, produced by chasing† and engraving the gold, shows a Savoyard entertainer playing the *musette* (bagpipes) while he manipulates a pair of puppets with his foot.

Gold boxes were made and fitted together by goldsmiths but much of the decoration was undertaken by craftsmen from other guilds, such as chasers, engravers and enamellers. The whole process, from commission to delivery to the customer, might take two years.

Louis Roucel, Snuff box
French 1766-7 (3.9 x 7.9 x 5.7cm)

Johann-Christian Neuber, Snuff box
German c.1770-5 (3.5 x 8.3 x 5.8cm)

Boxes were often enamelled with miniature reproductions of famous paintings of the day, known from Salon† exhibitions and engravings. The scenes on the Roucel box are after paintings by Greuze, with his *Village Wedding* on the cover.

The gold and cornelian† box by Neuber has Leda† and the Swan in relief on the lid. In the base is a secret slide with, on each side, gouache† miniature portraits of Voltaire† and his mistress, the marquise du Châtelet. Voltaire commissioned the box after the marquise du Châtelet's death, probably as a keepsake of his love.

There are also boxes decorated with Sèvres porcelain,† Japanese lacquer,† tortoiseshell *piqué*,† mother-of-pearl, diamonds and hard stones such as lapis lazuli and rock crystal.

Snuff boxes, airtight when closed, are precisely balanced so that they can be held open in the palm of the hand without tipping. Their size and weight suggest they were for display as much as wear. Snuff was taken by men and women and was subject to complex etiquette. A French pamphlet of c.1750 lists 14 steps including '(9) Take a clean pinch in your right hand. (10) Hold for some time before taking to the nose... (12) Sniff judiciously with both nostrils and without grimacing. (13) Sneeze, cough and spit.'

Silver-gilt service, Augsburg 1757-73
(large mirror: 83 x 56cm)

In 1773, it would not have seemed incredible for a very fine lady to have need of fifty-five pieces of silver-gilt† in order to rise, partake of a light breakfast and write a short letter. This service, probably given as a betrothal or wedding present, would have been on show when its owner performed her morning toilette before an audience of favoured guests.

Antoine-Nicolas Martinière, Perpetual almanac, French 1741-2 (46 x 31.8cm)

The capacity of the perpetual almanac to predict the exact order of time for eternity would have seemed quite magical when it was made for Louis XV by the enameller, Martinière. The twelve months are split between four gilt-bronze frames which bear dedications to the King. Each month has three columns containing plaques, made of copper, on which are painted in enamel the phases of the moon, the days of the week, the dates, the month, the nearest sign of the Zodiac, and the Saints' days and feast and fast days of the Church. The frames have removable brass backs so that the plaques can be adjusted at the end of the year.

The West Room was Lady Wallace's bedroom. It is decorated with fine paintings by Boucher and some exquisite examples of Louis XVI furniture.

François Boucher *Madame de Pompadour* French 1759 (91 x 68cm)

Jeanne-Antoinette Poisson (1721-64) was a Parisian commoner. She married and had two children before becoming the mistress of Louis XV. In 1745 she was created marquise de Pompadour and Mistress to the King, an official position invented by Louis XIV. She shared with the King a passion for architecture and the arts. In 1763, the 1st Marquess met Madame de Pompadour in Paris. He described her as 'most polite and obliging, with a great deal more sense and conversation than I had expected.'

Studio of Van Loo *Louis XV* French c.1759 (136.6 x 104cm)

Madame de Pompadour stands in a garden accompanied by her spaniel, Inès. A contemporary described Madame de Pompadour, 'Her eyes have a particular charm which perhaps derives from their uncertain colour ...' The setting evokes the park at Bellevue, Madame de Pompadour's château, where 'roses, jasmine and even orange trees ... seemed to spring from the bosom of the earth.' By 1759, Madame de Pompadour's relationship with the King was platonic, a state of affairs referred to by the statue, *Friendship Consoling Love*. Madame de Pompadour's fidelity is emphasised by her dog: as Inès is faithful to her mistress, so her mistress is faithful to the King.

Van Loo painted a state portrait of the King and then made a reduced-size replica to be used as a model by copyists. Numerous copies, of which this painting is an example, were given by the King to foreign royalty, and loyal friends and relations. One was owned by Madame de Pompadour.

François Boucher
Venus and Vulcan
French 1754 (164 x 76.6cm)

François Boucher
Mars and Venus Surprised by Vulcan
French 1754 (164 x 76.6cm)

François Boucher
The Judgement of Paris
French 1754 (164 x 76.6cm)

Venus and Vulcan shows Venus, goddess of love, and her husband, Vulcan, god of fire and smith and armourer to the gods, in Vulcan's forge. Cupid, son of Venus, sharpens his arrows on the anvil while Vulcan is distracted by Venus.

In *Mars and Venus Surprised*, Vulcan catches his wife with her lover, Mars – notice how Venus has contrived to tie a ribbon in the god of war's hair. Vulcan, hearing of his wife's infidelity, forged a golden net to entrap the lovers and invited the other gods to enjoy their humiliation. But the plan backfired when the voyeurs Neptune, god of the sea, and Mercury, messenger of the gods, were themselves bewitched by the charms of the naked Venus.

In *The Judgement of Paris*, the shepherd Paris must award the golden apple to the fairest of Venus, Juno, queen of the gods, and Minerva, goddess of wisdom. Venus bribes Paris by promising him the love of the most beautiful woman in the world and Paris gives the prize to Venus. In typical fashion, Boucher ignores the moral implications of the myth in order to concentrate on portraying three naked women from different angles.

Boucher (1703-70) epitomised the inimitable style of mid 18th-century French art at a time when most of Europe sought to follow the French Court and Paris. In his later years his work attracted criticism at the Salon,[†] but his career did not suffer because from 1750 he benefited from the lavish patronage of Madame de Pompadour. Boucher also created designs for tapestries, stage sets and porcelain groups. In 1755, he became the artistic director in charge of design at the Gobelins tapestry factory.

Pierre Gouthière and others *The Avignon Clock*
French 1771 (68.5 x 59 x 33.8cm)

The Avignon Clock is a gilt-bronze†
mantel clock. A personification
of the city of Avignon stands to
the left of the dial crowning the
coronet and coat of arms of
the marquis de Rochechouart.
He was governor of Avignon for
six years until 1774, when the
city was handed back to the Pope
by Louis XV. The citizens were
so delighted with the marquis'
governorship that they gave him
The Avignon Clock. Avignon
is recognisable by her crown,
made from the walls of the city.
Beneath her, personifications of
the river Rhône and the river
Durance, which join west of the
city, recline on a rocky hill with
river water flowing from their urns.
The Rhône, on the left, appears
to be in conversation with the
youthful Durance, who bends
and uproots a sapling with the
force of her current.

The case of *The Avignon Clock* was designed by the sculptor Boizot. It was
cast, chased† and gilded by Gouthière, a gilder on metal. The movement is
by Delunésy. The dial was painted with enamel and fired by the enameller,
Coteau. Gouthière was paid six times as much as Boizot and twenty-five
times as much as Delunésy, reflecting the relative importance of casting,
chasing and gilding in the production of such a clock.

Pierre Gouthière and others
Perfume burner, French 1774-5 (48.3 x 21.7cm)

The perfume burner is an
outstanding example of the
work of Gouthière. A gilt-bronze
serpent twists through the legs
of the gilt-bronze tripod which
supports a red jasper† bowl.
The perfume burner was in the
possession of Marie-Antoinette
in 1783, the year in which
her large inner apartment at
Versailles was redecorated
with white and gold panelling
incorporating gilded carvings
of perfume burners on tripods
with aromatic smoke wafting
from their bowls.

Gouthière (1732-1812/14)
was the greatest gilder
on metal of the Louis XVI
period. He perfected a
new process of gilding
whereby parts of a gilt
bronze could be given
a matt finish to contrast
with the burnished parts.

When the French Revolution
began, Marie-Antoinette tried
to safeguard her treasures,
including the perfume burner,
by entrusting them to various
Parisian shopkeepers and
dealers who had served her.
Her actions were in vain as
she was executed in 1793.

Adam Weisweiler, Work table
1786-90 (76.5 x 65.8 x 38.5cm)

The Empress Josephine, wife of
the Emperor Napoleon I, might
have kept her silk threads and
fabrics on the different tiers of
the work table, which belonged
to her in the 1800s. The table is
veneered with satinwood[†] laid
in diamond-shapes and inlaid
with dots of ebony.[†] The table
is mounted with Wedgwood
jasper-ware[†] cameos showing
white figures against pale-blue
backgrounds. The subjects are
derived from classical mythology;
on the front Cupids play (notice
the game of Blind Man's Buff on
the bottom tier).

Weisweiler (1744-1820), a German,
settled in Paris during the reign
of Louis XVI. He specialised in small
pieces of furniture of light, almost fragile,
appearance, designed for use by ladies.

René Dubois
Commode (chest of drawers)
French c.1760 (92 x 157.5 x 57cm)

Dubois, Commode, detail

The Dubois commode has a single drawer in front and two side
cupboards. The eccentric mix of neo-classical elements, such
as sirens, and oriental elements, such as Chinese fretwork and
Japanese lacquer,[†] is typical of the period. The lacquer, dyed
black, has been built up in relief and gilded.

Lacquer wares were imported
into Europe from China and
Japan and pieces of lacquer
were often incorporated into
European furniture. Lacquer
was extremely expensive and
was reused in new pieces
of furniture. In consequence,
pieces which originally
belonged to different panels
were sometimes jumbled
together in a collage. If you
look at the drawer front of
the Dubois commode, you
will see that it is made up of
small pieces which bear no
relation to each other. Dubois
has used the gilt-bronze
fretwork to hide the joins.

The West Gallery is a testament to the particular passion of the 4th Marquess. It contains one of the most important collections of French 18th-century paintings in the world. Several of the pieces of furniture were made for Marie-Antoinette and exquisite miniatures dating from the 16th to 18th centuries are displayed in the centre cases.

Peter Adolf Hall *The Painter's Family* French c.1776 (9 x 11cm)

Harriette Wilson, celebrated courtesan, visited Seamore Place, London home of the 3rd Marquess, and wrote that 'after dinner, he showed us miniatures, by the most celebrated artists, of at least half a hundred lovely women, black, brown, fair and even carrotty, for the amateur's sympathetic *bonne bouche...*'

The Painter's Family shows Hall's wife, Adélaïde, on the left and his sister-in-law on the right. His 4 year old daughter lies in her mother's lap. Hall was born in Sweden and settled in Paris where he built up a reputation as the leading miniaturist. *The Painter's Family* is one of his masterpieces and Richard Wallace paid a very high price for it.

The *Portrait of Holbein* is painted on vellum[†] laid on a 16th-century playing card; two hearts are just visible. Horenbout, a leading miniaturist of the Ghent-Bruges school, was appointed King's Painter to Henry VIII of England in 1534. In his service he became the friend and teacher of Hans Holbein, who is shown painting with a paint pot in his left hand.

Lucas Horenbout *Portrait of Holbein* English 1543 (4.2 x 4.2cm)

Louis-Nicolas and Henri-Joseph van
Blarenberghe *View of the Château
de Romainville* French 1782
(5.2 x 7.5cm), set in a gold box

View of the Château de Romainville is painted in gouache[†] on
vellum and installed on the cover of a gold box constructed 1781-3.
Five more views of the château and its famous anglo-chinois gardens
appear on the remaining sides of the box. The marquis de Ségur,
owner of the château, founded a society which made an annual award
of a dowry for marriage to a deserving young village girl. The miniature
shows the marquis and members of his family welcoming the girl.

Ascribed to Leleu, Toilet and writing table
French c.1763-4 (70.8 x 57 x 43.7cm)

The toilet and writing table would have been used by a lady to make her
toilette and write her morning letters. The compartments were for
writing materials, scent bottles, pomade pots, brushes and so on.
It was made in the workshop of Oeben and shows the mechanical
ingenuity which he introduced into late Louis XV furniture. The table
top depicts a naturalistic basket of flowers, assembled from several
pieces of veneer and engraved to show the veining of the leaves and petals.

Jean-Antoine Watteau *The Music Party* French c.1718 (67.3 x 94.8cm)

In *The Music Party*, a woman plays the guitar on a palatial terrace;
a man leans proprietorially against her chair. In the centre another
man tunes a large lute in preparation for making love to the seated lady
by playing and singing to her. But the longer he takes to tune his lute,
the greater the chance he gives his rival to win the favour of the lady.
Watteau was fascinated by such moments of emotional suspense.

The Rotunda at 2 rue Laffitte
(4th Marquess' apartment) c.1903

The 4th Marquess bought 18th-century French
paintings with a compulsion bordering on obsession.
He was highly intelligent but prey to neurosis and
hypochondria and he avoided public life. He lived in an
apartment in the rue Laffitte, Paris, surrounded by his
French pictures. It was written that he 'would not even
have drawn back his curtain to see a revolution go past
in the street.' Only the art of the *ancien régime*,[†] so
lightly touched by the cares of function and necessity,
satisfied his yearning for art that was 'pleasing'
and 'pretty'.

Jean-Antoine Watteau *Harlequin and Columbine* French c.1716-18 (36 x 24.9cm)

Watteau (1684-1721) gave expression to a new atmosphere in early 18th-century Paris. His synthesis of Rubensian colour and naturalistic observation fitted perfectly the new taste for small and intimate works suitable for the less formal rooms of the period. His elegant and amorous outdoor companies, or *fêtes galantes*, were a fresh genre in Paris. Watteau delighted in *commedia dell'arte*, the ribald comedy of carnival tradition which started as a popular entertainment in early 16th-century Italy. Its stock characters, including Harlequin, Columbine and Mezzetin, take part in absurd and witty plots wearing costumes and masks. Watteau happily mixed theatrical and contemporary costumes and his critics accused him of painting pictures with no subject.

Harlequin and Columbine shows Columbine recoiling from Harlequin's advances. Behind them a guitarist plays and a seated couple follow a musical score. The *commedia dell'arte* characters Pierrot and Crispin are in the background. Harlequin's inopportune love-making is expressed by his demoniac emergence from the shadows and his awkward lunge.

In *Gilles and his Family*, the central figure is dressed in the costume of the *commedia dell'arte* character, Mezzetin, the rascally valet, musician and rival of Harlequin. His libidinous character is suggested by the sculpted faun above his head.

Jean-Antoine Watteau *Gilles and his Family* French c.1716-18 (27.1 x 19cm)

Jean-Honoré Fragonard *The Swing*
French 1767 (81 x 64.2cm)

The Swing is Fragonard's most famous painting. One critic wrote, 'the grace of its execution and the tact of the artist excuse the sauciness of the subject.' A tantalising girl, delicious in her froth of pink silk, is poised in mid-air beyond the reach of both her elderly husband and her glowing lover. The fantastical park-landscape provides an ideal setting. A statue of *Love* makes the viewer party to the adulterous deception by holding his finger to his lips. The flirtatiously discarded slipper adds the perfect note of artful abandon.

The dramatist Collé related the amusing story behind *The Swing*: the history painter Doyen was summoned by an unnamed 'gentleman of the Court' to attend him at his pleasure house. The gentleman pointed to his mistress and said 'I should like you to paint Madame on a swing pushed by a bishop. Myself you will place in a position where I can observe this charming girl's legs, and more still if you wish to enliven your picture further.' Doyen was rendered speechless by this libertine proposal. However, he recovered sufficiently to suggest that the picture would be rendered yet more agreeable by the addition of Madame's slippers flying through the air, and that Fragonard, rather than himself, would be the best man for the job. (Fragonard does not in the end make any reference to the Church in his composition.) The identity of the racy patron who adores his mistress from the undergrowth is uncertain. The first known owner of *The Swing* was the receiver general, Ménage de Pressigny, who was guillotined in 1794.

Jean-Honoré Fragonard *The Souvenir*
French c.1776-8 (25.2 x 19cm)

Jean-Honoré Fragonard *Le petit parc*
French c.1764-5 (36.6 x 45cm)

In *The Souvenir* a girl carves her lover's initial, 'S', on a tree. She is observed by her spaniel, a symbol of steadfast fidelity. Notice the girl's delicately drawn profile, the calligraphic traceries of hair and foliage and the theatrical lighting. The use of panel, the scale and the careful technique show Fragonard catering for the 18th-century taste for the 'little masters' of the 17th-century Netherlands.

Fragonard spent the summer of 1760 sketching in the gardens of the Villa d'Este, Tivoli,[†] which had grown wild. His friend remarked 'Fragonard is all on fire; his drawings are very numerous; one cannot wait for another; they enchant me. I find in them some sort of sorcery.' The dilapidated charm of the gardens inspired Fragonard to paint a series of pictures of which *Le petit parc* is the finest.

Fragonard (1732-1806) studied under Boucher in Paris. He was one of the most versatile and brilliant artists of 18th-century France. Some critics accused him of compromising his artistic integrity by pandering to the frivolous tastes of collectors rather than pursuing history painting, for which he had been highly commended.

Secretaire (open), detail

The Petit Trianon is a small pavilion next
to Versailles. It was built by Louis XV,
on the advice of Madame de Pompadour,
and Louis XVI gave it to Marie-Antoinette.
She occupied an apartment on the
main floor and rearranged the gardens.
Artificial hills, grottoes and lakes were
linked by winding footpaths with charming
buildings around every corner. There
was even a hamlet complete with twelve
peasant houses and a mill with an
operational waterwheel.

Jean-Henri Riesener
Secretaire (writing desk)
French 1783 (139.6 x 80.5 x 42cm)

The secretaire was supplied by Riesener for Marie-Antoinette at
the Petit Trianon. The front drops down to form a writing surface
and papers can be kept secret (hence '*secrétaire*') in drawers and
compartments concealed behind the doors. The reduced dimensions
of the secretaire reflect the small size of the Petit Trianon. Richest
of all the Riesener furniture in the West Gallery, the secretaire is
veneered with a stunning fret pattern enclosing holly inlaid with
waterlilies of stained sycamore. The gilt-bronze[†] plaque on the
drop-front represents a Sacrifice to Love: a kneeling woman presents
an infant to Cupid, who stands on a pedestal with smoke from the
brazier on the lower step winding behind him. The gilt-bronze plaque
on the top drawer shows two naked infants sitting on clouds by
a brazier. One strokes a spaniel while the other holds out a letter
to Mercury, messenger of the gods, who wears a winged cap and
ties winged sandals to his feet.

The dauphin Louis, grandson
of Louis XV, married
Marie-Antoinette, the 15 year
old daughter of the Austrian
Empress. Louis ascended
the throne in 1774 aged 20.
Although kind-hearted and
well-intentioned, the King
lacked the intellect and
character necessary to
deal with the mounting
crisis of the *ancien régime*.
His frivolous and extravagant
wife was very unpopular
which harmed the prestige
of the monarchy. In 1793,
four years after the start of
the French Revolution, the
infamous guillotine sliced off
the heads of its most elevated
victims, the King and Queen.

M any of the painters represented in the Nineteenth-
Century Gallery belonged to the artistic and literary
salon society of 19th-century Paris; they were
contemporaries of the 4th Marquess and Richard Wallace.
The first half of the century was the age of romanticism, which
turned away from the 18th-century faith in the power of reason.
Artists looked to the past, to the cultures of distant lands and
to the natural world for inspiration and guidance. This gave
rise to an unprecedented diversity of subject matter.

Jean-Baptiste Isabey
Madame Dugazon French 1813
(12.5 x 9.5cm)

Attributed to Jean-Baptiste
Isabey *Self-portrait*
French c.1800-5 (16.3 x 12.6cm)

Madame Dugazon is a portrait
of a famous actress. Her face,
wearing a melancholy smile,
is wreathed in diaphanous veils
which flutter in an imaginary
breeze. This fashionable look
was created by Isabey.

Isabey (1767-1855) was the leading
portrait miniaturist of the Napoleonic
era. He took an active part in Paris social
life and was much sought after by the
philosopher and writer Mme de Staël for
her salon. He was introduced to Napoleon
by a pupil at the school where he taught
drawing and became his Court Painter in
1804. Official patronage was continued by
Louis XVIII, Charles X and Louis-Philippe.

The word 'romantic' was
drawn from the medieval
literary form, the 'romance'.
Romanticism turned the
irrational and fantastic
qualities of these tales into
positive values. It embodied
the belief that there are
crucial areas of human
experience neglected by the
rational mind and stressed
the importance of emotion,
intuition and imagination.

Ary Scheffer *Francesca da Rimini*
French 1835 (166.5 x 234)

The subject of *Francesca da Rimini* is taken from Dante's *Inferno*, a medieval epic poem. Dante makes a journey through hell with Virgil, the Roman poet, as his guide. They come upon the tragic figures of Paolo and Francesca, who are condemned to the stormy darkness of Hell's second circle with the other souls of the lustful. Francesca had been forced into marriage with the hideous Gianciotto da Rimini but fell in love with his younger brother, Paolo. Gianciotto caught the lovers while they were reading the romance *Sir Launcelot and Queen Guinevere*. He stabbed them both to death – their stab wounds are clearly visible.

The remarkable frame was made for Demidoff, who bought *Francesca da Rimini* in 1853. At the top is the inferno of Hell; in the corners are arrows and flaming torches, symbols of love. At the bottom are the towers of Rimini; in the corners are a chain ring, for eternal love, and the book which Paolo and Francesca were reading. Around the frame are parts of Dante's text.

$\mathcal{A}$ Anatole Demidoff, Prince of San Donato, was a contemporary of the 4th Marquess. They were two of the most extravagant collectors of the Second Empire (the reign of Napoleon III, Emperor of the French 1852-70). The 4th Marquess was a friend and supporter of Napoleon III, whose son used to ride his pony in the grounds of the 4th Marquess' château de Bagatelle in the Bois de Boulogne outside Paris. Demidoff owned a grand villa at San Donato, on the outskirts of Florence. In the last decade of his life he began to sell parts of his collection and the 4th Marquess acquired many of his finest works of art.

Horace Vernet *The Dog of the Regiment Wounded*
French 1819 (53.1 x 64.3cm)

Horace Vernet *The Wounded Trumpeter*
French 1819 (53.1 x 64.4cm)

The pair of pictures by Vernet were immensely popular when they were painted. It was said that engravings were 'in every shop window.' *The Dog of the Regiment Wounded* depicts a bugler and a drummer tending to the wounded dog. Behind them thick clouds of gunpowder smoke show that the battle still rages. In *The Wounded Trumpeter*, a soldier lies helpless, his trumpet by his side. His horse and his dog, invested with human sentiment, keep watch over him.

Jean-Baptiste Isabey
The Duke of Wellington
French 1818 (14.2 x 10.8cm)

Jean-Baptiste Isabey *Napoleon I*
French 1810 (21.5 x 17cm)

Jean-Baptiste Isabey
The Empress Josephine
French 1804-9 (13.5 x 9.4cm)

Jean-Baptiste Isabey
The Empress Marie-Louise and her son
French 1815 (17 x 13cm)

Napoleon Bonaparte (1769-1821) had a meteoric rise to power. He entered the French army when he was 16 and, in 1804 aged 35, he was created Emperor of the French. He was finally defeated by the Duke of Wellington and the Prussians at the Battle of Waterloo in 1815. He divorced his first wife, Josephine, because she had failed to produce an heir. His second wife was Marie-Louise, daughter of the Austrian Emperor and great-niece of Marie-Antoinette. She bore him a son, 'The King of Rome'.

Ernest Meissonier *The Roadside Inn* French 1865 (22.4 x 19.1cm)

In Meissonier's lifetime, the social and financial élites of Paris paid huge prices for his diminutive panels. They bought directly from the artist and at auction. Early collectors included the 4th Marquess, Napoleon III, and Richard Wallace.

Ernest Meissonier *Polichinelle* French 1860 (55.2 x 36cm)

The Roadside Inn shows horsemen in Louis XV costume stopping at an inn for refreshments. Midday sun shines through the foliage. The sharp, bright colours and dappled shadows give the painting a sparkling, effervescent quality.

An Artist Showing his Work depicts an artist, in a black coat, showing his work to a gentleman. Both wear Louis XV costume. The paintings on the walls are by Meissonier himself: there is a self-portrait in the upper centre.

The figure *Polichinelle* (Punch) was painted on a door in Madame Sabatier's hôtel in Paris. When she sold her collection, the panel was cut from the door and was bought by the 4th Marquess.

Ernest Meissonier *An Artist Showing his Work* French 1850 (37.5 x 29.1cm)

Meissonier (1815-91) was inspired by 17th-century Dutch paintings. Many critics exclaimed at the 'microscopic' perfection of the artist's 'Lilliputian' gallery. Meissonier said, 'Nowadays the only thing left for a painter is to show people the past as it was.' He owned historical costumes and a collection of arms and armour.

In the 1850s, Richard Wallace frequented the salon of the beautiful Madame Sabatier (it is said that she became his mistress in 1860). There he would have associated with, among others, his friend Meissonier, the poet Baudelaire and the novelist Flaubert.

In the first decades of the 19th century, the East Drawing Room was Isabella, Marchioness of Hertford's sitting room. Here she entertained the Prince Regent during his daily visits which lasted throughout their liaison, 1807-20. The Prince (later George IV) was besotted with the middle-aged Marchioness, though she never became his mistress. At the time the room was furnished with salmon-coloured silk curtains, white and gold seat furniture and Isabella's collection of Sèvres porcelain.

Hertford House in 1813 (Wallace Collection Archives)

'Through M-nch-st-r Square took a canter just now –
Met the *old yellow chariot*, and made a low bow.
This I did, of course, thinking 'twas loyal and civil,
But got such a look – oh 'twas black as the devil!
How unlucky! – *incog.* he was trav'lling about,
And I, like a noodle, must go find him out!
Mem. – when next by the old yellow chariot I ride,
To remember there *is* nothing Princely inside.'

(Thomas Moore 'Wednesday' from *Extracts from the Diary of a Politician* in *Intercepted Letters: the Twopenny Postbag and Trifles*, 8th ed. 1813)

The Bacchic theme, veneered in brass and tortoiseshell Boulle marquetry on the back of the mirror, is unfortunately appropriate to its first owner's intemperance. Notice the monkey which dangles a mouse just out of reach of a cat while another teases a dog with a bone. The design derives from an engraving after Jean Berain.

Berain (1637-1711), French engraver and ornamental designer, was one of the creators of Louis XIV-style ornament. In 1674 he became the Designer of the King's Bedroom and Cabinet. He made full use of the arabesque[†] and the grotesque.[†]

Attributed to André-Charles Boulle, Toilet mirror, the back, French 1713 (73 x 56cm)

The infamous duchesse de Berry would have arranged her wig and applied her face-patches in the toilet mirror which was part of a toilet service. The duchesse was married to Louis XIV's third grandson. Her lady-in-waiting was the wife of the duc de Saint-Simon.[†] He described the duchesse in his *Mémoires* as 'a model of all the vices.'

André-Charles Boulle
Console table, the top
French c.1705 (81.4 x 56cm)

Console table, side view

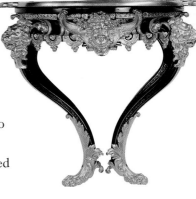

The console table was designed to stand against a wall between two windows. On its top, two tight-rope walking monkeys attempt to dislodge hanging bunches of grapes. One, in waistcoat and feathered cap, advances confidently while the other wobbles.

Willem Drost *Young Woman in a Brocade Gown*
Dutch c.1654 (62.4 x 49.8cm)

Govaert Flinck *A Young Archer* Dutch c.1639-40 (66.2 x 50.8cm)

Drost was a pupil in Rembrandt's Amsterdam studio in or shortly before 1650. He was able to switch between his master's virtuoso style of the 1650s, with its broad, loose touch and increasingly sharp contrasts of light and dark, and the more fashionable refined and highly-finished style which he uses in *Young Woman in a Brocade Gown*.

Flinck trained in Leeuwarden before going to Amsterdam in 1633, aged 17, to join Rembrandt's studio. He set up as an independent master 3 years later. Bol trained in Dordrecht before joining Rembrandt's studio in 1637, aged 19. He set up on his own 5 years later. Both Flinck and Bol were heavily influenced by their master for many years after leaving his studio.

Ferdinand Bol *The Toper* Dutch c.1650-1 (89.2 x 82.3cm)

Tronies are character studies of heads in exotic dress, a genre developed by Rembrandt and Jan Lievens in their Leiden studio, 1626-31. *The Toper* (drinker or drunkard), shown in 16th-century costume wearing a gold medallion with St George, patron saint of soldiers, is a good example. *The Young Archer* may be a *tronie* or he may be a specific character; the same subject appears in a print by Jan de Visscher with an inscription, 'Thus the Moor with bow and arrow has the foe or the game in sight.'

In East Galleries I hang some of nearly two hundred 17th-century Netherlandish paintings in the Wallace Collection. Here you may test your skills of connoisseurship – is it, or is it not, by Rembrandt? – and compare paintings and workshop practices in the northern and southern Netherlands at a fascinating period of their history.

When the 4th Marquess died in August 1870, his will was locked in a drawer of a writing-table at Bagatelle, his château in the Bois de Boulogne. He left the residue of all his real and personal estate to Richard Wallace 'for all his care and attention to my Dear Mother and likewise for his devotedness to me during a long and painful illness ...' The will took everyone by surprise as the 4th Marquess had never publicly recognised Wallace as his son. The property included the art collections in London and Paris, the rue Laffitte apartment and Bagatelle in Paris, 105 Piccadilly in London and a considerable estate in Ireland. The East Galleries were built in 1872-5 to help display the enormous collection Wallace now owned.

David Teniers the Younger *The Smokers* Flemish 1644 (36.5 x 50.2cm)

At the beginning of the 17th century the Netherlands (now Holland and Belgium) belonged to Spain and were ruled from a court in Brussels by governors sent from Spain. Protestant rebellions broke out all over the country before the beginning of the century. In 1609 the Dutch north broke away from the Flemish south and reached a truce with the Spanish Governors. War broke out again in 1612 and did not end until 1648 when the north officially split from the south.

Adriaen Brouwer *A Peasant Asleep* Flemish c.1635-6 (36.6 x 27.6cm)

A Peasant Asleep, The Smokers and *A Riverside Inn* are called 'low life' genre, which, curiously, was highly sought after in the decadent world of 18th-century France. *The Smokers* is a study of smoking. A man rolls tobacco in a paper; a second stuffs his pipe; a third draws on his lit pipe. Smoking was considered a vice in the 17th-century Netherlands, especially when indulged in by peasants.

The simple composition, delicate colouring and bravura handling of *A Peasant Asleep* is typical of Brouwer. Brouwer worked in Haarlem alongside Hals until he moved to Antwerp in 1631 where he influenced Teniers. Rubens owned seventeen of Brouwer's works and Rembrandt owned six.

A Riverside Inn shows a party of peasants sitting around a barrel outside an inn. In 1832, this painting was called 'The diamond,' a tribute to its fresh execution. It reveals an Arcadian[†] spirit, a more positive attitude to peasant life than the satirical *A Peasant Asleep* and *The Smokers*. It is typical of scenes reproduced as decoration on luxury commodities of the *ancien régime*[†] such as Sèvres porcelain[†] vases and gold snuff boxes.

David Teniers the Younger *A Riverside Inn* Flemish, later 1640s (22.8 x 34.5cm)

Peter Paul Rubens *The Birth of Henri IV*
Flemish 1628 (21.5 x 37.2cm)

Peter Paul Rubens *The Union of Henri IV and Marie de Médicis*
Flemish 1628 (23 x 12.2cm)

The Birth and *The Union* (and *The Triumph of Henri IV*, also in this gallery) belong to a set of *modelli* prepared by Rubens for a series of twenty-four paintings, *The Life of Henri IV*. The series was commissioned by Marie de Médicis, the widow of Henri IV, King of France. (A series celebrating and glorifying Marie de Médicis' life had already been painted by Rubens.) Work on the full-size paintings was abandoned when Marie de Médicis fell out with her son, Louis XIII. She was exiled from France by Cardinal Richelieu in 1631. In *The Birth*, a personification of the city of Pau, the birthplace of Henri IV, nurses the baby who is presented with a sword by Mars, god of war. Beneath them reclines the god of the river which flows through Pau. In the sky is Sagittarius, the Zodiac sign for December, the month in which Henri IV was born. Henri IV married Marie de Médicis by proxy in Florence. *The Union* shows the King wearing a half-armour and holding an olive branch, concessions to his married state. The couple are watched over by Hymen, god of marriage.

Rubens' *modelli* were oil sketch designs for paintings. Assistants in Rubens' large Antwerp studio worked up the full-size painting from the *modello*. The degree of Rubens' participation varied from commission to commission – sometimes the whole painting, sometimes just finishing hands and faces – and customers were charged accordingly. Rubens' *modelli* are highly valued as the true work of the master's hand, showing the spontaneity of his thought processes as he drew with paint.

Attributed to Govert Flinck *Landscape with a Coach* Dutch c.1640 (47 x 66cm)

In *Landscape with a Coach*, the richly dressed man, attended by his servant and hounds, is perhaps a *vanitas*[†] figure. He faces the sun and sees a poor farm, a distant port and a castle; also a milkmaid, a ferryman, travellers, harvesters and a coachman. The different types of human endeavour are joined by the winding road, giving the impression of the progress of a human life. But all is vain for the day of judgement will come to everyone. 'Be prepared,' says the fortified castle. Notice the high viewpoint and the whimsical architecture.

The subject of *The Good Samaritan* is taken from the Gospel of St Luke. The Samaritan is at the top of the steps paying the innkeeper. He has brought to the inn a man who has been robbed and wounded. The Samaritan found the man lying in the roadside ignored by passers by.

In Rembrandt's thriving and unashamedly commercial Amsterdam studio, it was normal practice for the work of assistants to bear the name of the master (written by him or by the assistant), showing that the painting was a product of the studio.

Attributed to Rembrandt van Rijn *The Good Samaritan* Dutch 1630 (24 x 20cm)

In 1890 there were twelve Rembrandts in the Wallace Collection. By 1990, there was only one, *Titus* (in the Great Gallery). Of the twelve, three, including *The Good Samaritan* and *Landscape with a Coach*, were bought by the 3rd Marquess. The rest were bought by the 4th Marquess. They were both great connoisseurs but they did not have access to the illustrated catalogues which exist today. By the end of the 19th century, paintings began to be reattributed. The process accelerated with the work of the Rembrandt Research Project in Amsterdam. In 1968 it embarked on a rigorous re-examination of Rembrandt's paintings employing scientific tools such as paint analysis and dendochronology.[†]

Aert van der Neer *A Skating Scene* Dutch c.1655-60 (53.4 x 68cm)

A Skating Scene depicts the beautifully studied effects of a winter sunset. The low winter sun catches the houses on the right while those on the left are in deep shadow. Some men play *kolf* (forerunner of golf); a man in a red coat drives an elegant, gilded sledge pulled by a horse with red and white plumes. On the left is a navigation pole. Can you see the circular sheet of ice cut from a hole on the left?

If *A Skating Scene* is everything we expect from a Dutch view then *Rocky Landscape* is not: a cottage perches on a rocky escarpment overlooking a waterfall, not a sight often seen in Holland. Ruisdael, one of the greatest Dutch landscape painters, was influenced by Van Everdingen

Jacob van Ruisdael *Rocky Landscape* Dutch 1650s (102.8 x 125.2cm)

(whose work you can see in this gallery), who had travelled in Scandinavia and continued to paint mountainous scenes with torrents and waterfalls on his return to the Netherlands.

The 3rd Marquess' taste has been called the only redeeming feature of a man who was an example of undisguised debauchery. He made a distinct contribution to the collection of Dutch and Flemish paintings in the Wallace Collection. He favoured the highly-finished genre scenes, meticulous townscapes and Dutch Italianate landscapes which you see in the East Galleries.

Jan Steen *Celebrating the Birth* Dutch 1664 (87.7 x 107cm)

In 17th-century Holland the birth of a baby was celebrated with a party. This was supposed to be a sober affair but gatherings often became riotous and legislation was introduced to control them. *Celebrating the Birth* is one such riot. The new mother lies in bed at the top left corner of the painting; the apparent father holds the baby, wrapped in a red cloth. Another man, a self-portrait of Jan Steen, makes the sign of cuckold's horns behind the baby's head. The cuckold is further emasculated by the apron, keys and purse strings around his waist (domestic duties should be carried out by the mistress of the house). The warming pan, prominent in the foreground, alludes to a saying, 'the only warmth in the marriage bed is the warming pan.' Other sexual innuendoes are provided by the hanging sausage and the broken eggshells – 'cracking the eggs into the pan' was a euphemism for sexual intercourse. The general debauchery is confirmed by the pregnant woman on the left who is drinking herself into a stupor.

Celebrating the Birth, detail

Steen's message is 'do not behave like these comical fools who cannot control their animal urges, for they shall go to Hell.' Steen attracted criticism from one preacher who accused him of using morality as an excuse to paint lascivious images.

Caspar Netscher *The Lace Maker* Dutch 1662 (33 x 27cm)

'Genre' is sometimes translated as 'a scene from everyday life' because it depicts everyday people and does not seem to have a narrative or subject. Although these images make a virtue of recording the particular rather than the ideal, they are as artificially composed as any mythological painting. Genre paintings often carry witty meanings made all the more pertinent by a realistic style of painting. Naturalistic motifs carry metaphorical connotations which can function as a lesson. The artist's view on his lesson may be earnestly righteous, ambivalent or comical.

The Lace Maker carries the opposite message to the painting by Jan Steen. It says, 'Do behave like this!' A young woman sits in an immaculate interior. In Dutch 17th-century opinion, a woman was easily corrupted if left to her own devices. The home was the bedrock of the new Dutch republic and a corrupt wife meant a corrupt home which in turn could wreak havoc on society. Many tracts and manuals instructed women and their husbands on correct use of female time. Jacob Cats' *Marriage Manual*, 1625, lists six legitimate states of womanhood – maid, sweetheart, bride, wife, mother and widow – and the appropriate behaviour for each stage. The central motif on the woman's embroidered cap is derived from an emblem of clasped hands and doves which decorates the engraved frontispiece to Cats' book. According to Cats, signs of a virtuous housewife included a spotless domain and industrious lace-making.

How did the mussel shells lying on the floor escape the vigorous broom of this virtuous housewife? Because they are a symbol of her virtue. A Dutch poem of 1623 advises,

Do as the mussel does and stay in your shell,
Be happy indoors, and don't go beyond yourself;
For if you keep to your house long and well,
You remain inviolable, and always fresh, and white.

This also explains the woman's discarded shoes: she cannot leave the house without shoes.

A Boy Bringing Bread shows the physical meeting of public and domestic worlds. The housewife receives the boy who brings bread. Beyond them, through the open doorway, areas of public and private space are indicated with bands of light and shadow: first, the courtyard of the house, then the outer passage, the pavement, the canal, the pavement on the other side of the canal and another private house with a woman standing at the door.

Pieter de Hooch *A Boy Bringing Bread* Dutch c. 1660-3 (73.5 x 59cm)

A Lady Reading a Letter shows a girl sitting at a table reading a love letter. The carpet covering the table has been pushed aside for sewing, but the girl's work lies unattended in a basket at her side. The painting has a curious stillness, like a rain drop suspended in mid-air for a fraction of a second. While she studies her lover's words, we can study the girl, her earring, the curl of her hair, but not her thoughts.

Gerard ter Borch *A Lady Reading a Letter* Dutch, early 1660s (44.2 x 32.2cm)

Titian *Perseus and Andromeda* Italian 1553-62 (175 x 189.5cm) (in the Great Gallery)

The 3rd Marquess bought *Perseus and Andromeda* in 1815. It was painted for Philip II of Spain and in the 17th century it belonged to Van Dyck. You can see it in the Great Gallery at the end of the enfilade of the East Galleries. Below the Titian are a Boulle chest of drawers (French c.1710) and a bronze of *Hercules and the Arcadian Stag* (Italian, mid 17th-century cast of a model of the 1590s). Together with the Dutch cabinet pictures in the East Galleries, they give a strong indication of the taste of the 3rd Marquess.

Hunting was used as a metaphor for the chase between man and woman. In *The Sleeping Sportsman* the hunter is incapable of catching the girl, who stands expectantly with an empty glass at the open doorway. The sportsman slumps in an alcoholic stupor, a flagon at his feet. In his lap droops a pipe – a common phallic symbol. The girl looks at a second man. He leans from the window apparently about to steal the sportsman's bird, or rather his opportunity for dalliance with the girl – the Dutch word 'vogel' means 'bird', and 'vogelen' ('to bird') was used as a euphemism for sexual intercourse. The thief's gaze makes us accomplices in his mockery of the sleeping man.

Gabriel Metsu *The Sleeping Sportsman* Dutch c.1658-60 (40.3 x 34.9cm)

A View of Yarmouth 1818
(The 3rd Marquess of Hertford
as Earl Yarmouth, aged 41)
(Wallace Collection Archives)

A View of Yarmouth 1818
(The 3rd Marquess of Hertford
as Earl Yarmouth, aged 41)
(Wallace Collection Archives)

The 3rd Marquess bought and sold art in the London sale rooms during the first three decades of the 19th century. Like many British noblemen of the Regency period, he profited from the dispersal of the great European collections enforced by the French Revolution and the ensuing Napoleonic wars. He became a favourite of the Prince of Wales during the latter's liaison with his mother. He acted as the Prince's agent, buying many Dutch and Flemish pictures which are in the Royal Collection today. Unlike his son, the 4th Marquess, who accumulated paintings on a grand scale regardless of their ultimate location, the 3rd Marquess acquired pictures to furnish his own rooms. He lived first in a house in Seamore Place, described in 1821 by Mrs Arbuthnot in her journal as 'the prettiest small house that ever was seen; full of beautiful pictures and buhl [sic] and curious books.' St Dunstan's was built 1826-32 and the 3rd Marquess obtained the lease of Dorchester House, Park Lane, in 1829.

The Tent Room at St Dunstan's
(The Architectural Association)

The 3rd Marquess used St Dunstan's for entertaining. It was a lavish villa built in Regent's Park. It consisted of a classical building with an adjoining Tent Room. The Tent Room was draped with nearly 200 metres of rich rose satin and was hung with crimson and gold curtains. It contained six huge pier-glasses and a French 'self-acting organ.'

Jan van der Heyden *View of the Westerkerk, Amsterdam* Dutch 1667/8-72 (41.3 x 59.1cm)

The paintings by Van der Heyden and De Witte demonstrate the Dutchman's delight in celebrating what he saw with his eyes by describing it in paint. The Westerkerk, built 1620-21, is viewed from across the Keizersgracht in Amsterdam. The detail on the façade of the church and its reflection in the canal are magical. You can see every brick on the canal wall.

Interior of the Oude Kerk shows the north transept and choir of the church from an oblique angle. It is remarkable for its vivid naturalism.

Emanuel de Witte
Interior of the Oude Kerk, Delft
Dutch 1651 (60.5 x 44cm)

Dutch Italianate landscape ranges from idealised Arcadian landscape and actual Italian landscape to indigenous Dutch landscape given a dose of Italian sunshine. Such landscapes were painted by Dutch artists in the northern Netherlands. Some had travelled to Italy or Germany. Some never left their native land.

Adam Pynacker *Landscape with Animals* Dutch c. 1665 (117.5 x 102.5cm)

Jan Both *Italian Landscape* Dutch c.1645 (81.2 x 104.7cm)

Pynacker probably went to Italy in 1645-8 but his *Landscape with Animals* was painted in Amsterdam. The foreground is cast in dark shadow and the distance recedes in a hazy glow. Details are picked out with little pools of sharp sunlight – craggy bark, huge curling leaves, the tips of the goat's horns, a herdsman driving home his cattle at the end of the day.

Italian Landscape was painted in Utrecht after Both's return from Rome where he befriended and collaborated with the French painter, Claude. He adopted Claude's method of composition along diagonals and bathed his landscapes in a similar warm light. Travellers on the winding

Aelbert Cuyp *The Ferry Boat* Dutch, early 1650s (71.5 x 89.7cm)

road add to an impression of distance and time passing.

Cuyp never went to Italy. His *Ferry Boat* probably depicts the crossing of the river Maas at Cuyp's native Dordrecht, invested with atmospheric, early-morning light. A flat-bottomed ferry goes to pick up a horse and cart and other passengers waiting on the bank. The new wealth of the young Dutch Republic depended on the country's rivers and canals and ferry crossings became patriotic symbols. The boat in the foreground flies a Dutch flag.

The Great Gallery c.1890

'My collection is the result of my life' wrote the 4th Marquess in 1857. The 17th-century old master paintings which hang in the Great Gallery are proof of his great connoisseurship. In the mid 19th century, the fashion was for the art of the Renaissance but the 4th Marquess' tastes were different. He favoured pictures of the highest quality painted by the 17th and 18th-century artists who had been collected during the *ancien régime*.

The top line of paintings in the Great Gallery celebrates 17th-century Dutch and Flemish still-life painters. In the 19th century these paintings were used decoratively, almost like wallpaper.

Frans Snyders *Larder with a Page*
Flemish 1615-20 (125 x 198cm)

Peter Paul Rubens *The Rainbow Landscape* Flemish c.1636 (135.6 x 235cm)

The Rainbow Landscape shows a late summer afternoon on Rubens' country estate with peasants bringing in the harvest. This is an idealised vision of a real landscape. In 1635, the 58 year old Rubens, who lived in Antwerp, bought a country château at Elewijt, between Brussels and Antwerp. There he spent most of the end of his life with his pretty second wife, Hélène Fourment, whom he married in 1630 when she was 16. He celebrated his purchase and his delightful marriage with a pair of landscapes, painted for his own pleasure. The pendant[†] to *The Rainbow* is *Het Steen*, a view of the château in morning sunshine (National Gallery, London).

The Rainbow Landscape and *Het Steen* became separated in the 19th century and the latter was given to the National Gallery, London. When *The Rainbow* came up for sale in 1856, the National Gallery was keen to reunite the pair. They were decisively outbid by the 4th Marquess who paid the considerable sum of 4,550 guineas. The 4th Marquess' power in the sale room was legendary.

Rubens was deeply patriotic. By 1636 he had largely retired from political life except that he continued to lobby the Spanish Hapsburg rulers of the southern Netherlands. He urged them to bring an end to the conflict with the rebel north which had caused crippling damage, both physical and economic, to Antwerp and the surrounding countryside. *The Rainbow Landscape* reflects Rubens' love for his native countryside; the rainbow recalls the covenant made between God and Man after the Flood and the harvest is just reward for the labours of Rubens' countrymen.

Anthony van Dyck *Marie de Raet*
Flemish 1631 (213.3 x 114.5cm)

Anthony van Dyck *Philippe Le Roy*
Flemish 1630 (213.3 x 114.5cm)

Marie de Raet and *Philippe Le Roy* are ambitious in scale and intended to impress the viewer with the exalted social position of the people portrayed. Philippe Le Roy has all the trappings of a nobleman: fine clothes, an aristocratic pose, a sword and a hunting dog. His young wife is dressed as a fashionable member of the nobility. She clutches her fan, revealing charming innocence and vulnerability; her small dog adds a note of submissive femininity. Van Dyck had just returned from Italy, and was the latest fashion in Antwerp, when he painted these pictures. The portraits represent a marvellous collusion between artist and sitters. Van Dyck captures not only likeness but aspiration. He creates an image which matches Le Roy's ambition without making him appear *arriviste*.

Le Roy is the visual embodiment of courtly ideals as set out in contemporary etiquette books. In fact he was the illegitimate grandson of a successful gunpowder manufacturer. The purpose of his life was self-advancement and his inauspicious start was soon swept under the carpet. He bought land and feudal rights which entitled him to call himself 'Lord of Ravels'. In 1631, aged 35, he married the 16 year old Marie de Raet, a member of the land-owning classes.

Bartolomé Estebán Murillo *The Adoration of the Shepherds* Spanish c. 1665 (146.7 x 218.4cm)

The Adoration of the Shepherds depicts an episode in Christ's nativity. The shepherds are the first to recognise the infant Son of God. They bring doves, the traditional offering for purification after birth, and a bound lamb, symbolising Christ's sacrifice. The combination of visionary effects and realistic details, such as the shepherd's dirty foot, give the picture an immediacy typical of Murillo, whose paintings were particularly admired by the 4th Marquess.

Attributed to Roger Scabol after Martin Desjardins
Equestrian statuette of Louis XIV
French c.1700 (43.8cm high)

The bronze *Equestrian statuette of Louis XIV* shows the King wearing Roman military dress and a fashionable French full-bottomed wig. His horse is modelled on the Roman statue of the Emperor Marcus Aurelius. He holds a commander's baton and his saddlecloth is decorated with the sun, a reference to Louis XIV's style, the Sun King. The statuette is a reduction of a monument erected in the King's honour in Lyons in 1713 and destroyed during the French Revolution.

A Dance to the Music of Time represents Jupiter's gift of Bacchus, god of wine, to the world following complaints by the Seasons and Time about the harshness of human life. The dancing group represents the seasons: Autumn, who is Bacchus, is crowned with dry leaves, Winter has her hair in a cloth, Spring has her hair braided like ears of corn, and Summer is crowned with roses. On the right, Saturn, god of time, accompanies the dance on his lyre. On the left a two-headed term† depicts the youthful and mature Bacchus. Infants play with an hourglass and with bubbles, symbols of the shortness and fragility of life. Apollo, the sun god, drives his chariot across the sky to make the day, another reminder of the passing of time. The dancers can also be identified with the perpetual cycle of the human condition: Poverty (Autumn) leads to Labour (Winter) who leads to Riches (Spring), who leads to Pleasure (Summer). But an excess of pleasure leads back to poverty and the cycle starts again. Poussin was not interested in creating naturalistic effects but in the universal philosophical message.

Nicolas Poussin
*A Dance to the Music
of Time* French
c.1635-6 (82.5 x 104cm)

In classical mythology Hercules is the personification of physical strength and bravery. The gilt-bronze† group *Hercules and a Centaur* shows Hercules wrestling with Eurytion the centaur (half man and half horse). The centaur was to marry Deianeira, who had been Hercules' lover, but, on the wedding day, Hercules slew the centaur and carried off the bride.

Attributed to Ferdinando Tacca *Hercules and a Centaur* Italian, mid 17th century (68cm high)

Philippe de Champaigne
The Annunciation
French c.1643-8 (334 x 214.5cm)

The dramatic austerity of *The Annunciation* reflects Philippe de Champaigne's religious sympathies (he belonged to a rigorous Catholic sect). It shows the moment in St Luke's Gospel when the Angel Gabriel announces to Mary that the Holy Spirit, symbolised by the descending dove, will cause her to bear the Son of God. Mary's abandoned work basket and *prie-dieu* (praying stool) refer to apocryphal accounts that Mary was sewing, praying or studying the prophecy of Isaiah when the angel appeared.

Apollo and the Cumæan Sybil is one of Rosa's finest works. The eerie calm of the landscape creates a sense of foreboding in keeping with the melancholy story from Ovid's *Metamorphoses*.[†] Apollo fell in love with the Cumæan Sybil and offered her anything she desired. She asked for as many years of life as there were grains of dust in her hand. Apollo granted her wish but she still refused his advances. In retribution he denied her perpetual youth and she lived in increasing misery for over 700 years.

Salvator Rosa
Apollo and the Cumæan Sybil
Italian 1650s
(173.7 x 259.5cm)

Rembrandt *Titus*, detail

Rembrandt accentuates the texture of the paint on the canvas, making the image seem immediate and spontaneous. The restricted palette and contrasts of light and shadow give the illusion of a psychological connection between Titus and the viewer.

Rembrandt van Rijn *Titus* Dutch c.1657 (68.5 x 57.3cm)

Titus is a portrait by a father of his teenage son. It was painted the year after Rembrandt was declared bankrupt and the 15 year old Titus and his stepmother, Hendrickje Stoffels, were obliged to administer the production of Rembrandt's etchings and the sale of his pictures in order to comply with guild regulations. Titus is depicted in historical robes with a gold chain, recalling 16th-century Venetian portraits. Rembrandt sympathetically captures the young man's serious gaze.

Diego Velázquez *The Lady with a Fan*
Spanish c.1636-44 (95 x 70cm)

The Lady with a Fan is a portrait of an unknown woman. She is dressed in the Spanish fashion of the late 1630s and early 1640s. Her fan is probably *piqué*† work of gold and turtleshell. Notice the rosary hanging from her left wrist. The stillness of her gaze gives the painting a mysterious intensity. The closely observed features and the reappearance of the same model in other works by the artist imply that she was in the artist's immediate circle, possibly his wife or daughter, rather than a member of the Court in Madrid (where Velázquez had been Painter to King Philip IV since 1623).

Frans Hals *The Laughing Cavalier*, Dutch 1624 (83 x 67.3cm)

Hals *The Laughing Cavalier*, detail

Arrows, bees, flaming torches and lovers' knots are drawn from love-emblem books published in the Netherlands in the first half of the 17th century. Engraved illustrations were accompanied by short sayings or poems. Cupid aims his bow: once an arrow has pierced your heart, you are doomed to fall in love with the next creature to cross your path. Bees buzz: the honey in the hive is the sweetness of love, and the bees which sting you are the pain of love.

The inscription in the top right corner of *The Laughing Cavalier* tells us that the portrait was painted in 1624 and that the sitter was aged 26. Perhaps it was painted to celebrate this enigmatic young man's betrothal: symbols of love are depicted in the embroidery on his jacket. Notice Hals's astonishing display of technique: the sensitive depiction of the facial expression, which suggests that the man is party to an amusing secret, the defiant execution of the sheen of satin and the different treatments of lace – compare the delicate perfection of the cuffs with the bravura dash of the ruff.

Hals had been a successful portrait painter in Haarlem but by 1865, when this painting came up for sale, no one had heard of him. The 4th Marquess spotted the painting, called simply *Portrait of a Man*, and determined to have it. So did his friend, the baron de Rothschild, and they bid against each other. Hertford won the battle, but at a price more than six times the sale estimate. The fame of the portrait following its starring role in this sale helped reinstate Hals' reputation as a major artist and turned the painting into an icon. Its title, acquired in the aftermath of the sale, is as famous as the image despite its inaccuracy (the man is neither laughing nor a cavalier).

Nelly O'Brien was a well-known beauty and courtesan. She was a friend of Reynolds, who used her as a model for his 'fancy pictures'. When this portrait was painted, Nelly was enjoying the protection of the 3rd Viscount Bolingbroke.

Joshua Reynolds *Nelly O'Brien*
English c.1762-4 (126.3 x 110cm)

'Perdita' is a portrait of the actress, Mrs Mary Robinson. She sits in an atmospheric landscape with her dog. The painting was commissioned by the Prince of Wales in the same year that he made a financial settlement upon Mrs Robinson, 8 months after the end of their affair (and after 8 months of negotiation with her). The Prince had become infatuated with Mrs Robinson in 1779 when he saw her playing Perdita in Shakespeare's *The Winter's Tale* at the Drury Lane Theatre. He sent her a miniature of himself with a paper heart inside declaring eternal love. Mrs Robinson had the miniature set in diamonds (she holds it on her lap in the painting). But she was soon ousted by a new mistress.

Thomas Gainsborough
Mrs Robinson 'Perdita' English 1781
(233.7 x 153cm)

Jean-Urbain Guérin *Georgiana,
Duchess of Devonshire, and Lady
Elizabeth Foster* French c.1791
(9.4 x 7cm) (in the West Gallery)

Richard Cosway *Mrs Fitzherbert*
English 1790 (7.2 x 5.9cm)
(in the West Gallery)

John Downman *Isabella, 2nd
Marchioness of Hertford, as Lady
Beauchamp* (aged 21)
English 1781 (21 x 16.7cm)
(in the Watercolour Gallery)

The Prince of Wales (1762-1830) was in constant rebellion against his father,
George III. At an early age he dived into a whirl of pleasure and annoyed the
King with his choice of friends and his politics. Under the auspices of Georgiana,
Duchess of Devonshire, he posed as a patron of the Whigs. He fell madly in love with
Mrs Fitzherbert, a Roman Catholic widow, and married her secretly in 1785, putting
in jeopardy his accession to the throne. In 1806 the Prince became acquainted,
through Mrs Fitzherbert, with Isabella, wife of the 2nd Marquess of Hertford.
In 1811 he became Prince Regent, when his father was declared insane, and ended
his connection with Mrs Fitzherbert. But as early as 1807 Joseph Farington wrote in
his diary: 'Mrs Fitzherbert has lost her influence over the P. He is now devoted to the
M-ss of H-d; to whom while they were in London He constantly went every day and
staid from three o clock till 5 ... I remarked that the M-ss is not young; she [Lady
Thomond] replied that notwithstanding she is an extraordinarily fine woman, a Juno.'
The Marchioness was then a middle-aged woman of 47.

Manchester Square Cattle Shew, 1812
(Wallace Collection Archives)

The Prince of Wales'
liaisons were viciously
satirised in the media. The
raging bull is the Prince, the
2nd Marchioness of Hertford
is the cow, and the 2nd
Marquess is the docile bull
with blunt horns. The Prince
flattered the 2nd Marquess
by including him in his favours.
In 1818 he gave the 2nd
Marquess Gainsborough's
Mrs Robinson which hangs
in the Great Gallery.

Lawrence was appointed Principal Painter to George IV on the death of Reynolds in 1792. The King gave this portrait to his mistress, Lady Conyngham. Lawrence considered it his 'most successful resemblance' of the King. Becky Sharp, in Thackeray's *Vanity Fair* (1848), describes the portrait as 'the famous one ... in a frock coat with a fur collar, and breeches and silk stockings, simpering on a sofa from under his curly brown wig.'

Thomas Lawrence *George IV* English 1822
(270.5 x 179cm)

In 1820 the Prince Regent succeeded to the throne. He grew tired of the 2nd Marchioness and began an affair with Lady Conyngham. The young Lord Beauchamp (later 4th Marquess) accurately summed up the situation after seeing the King riding with Lady Conyngham in Hyde Park: 'By G. our Grandmother must learn to ride or it is all over with us.' The King's portrait hangs on the wall beside Lady Conyngham, who plays with a sovereign, both gold and human varieties.

A Sketch of a Lady-Playing With A-Sovereign, 1829
(Wallace Collection Archives)

Lower
Ground Floor

In the Watercolour Gallery you can see the finest collection of watercolours by Bonington in the world and other superb 19th-century French and English watercolours.

Richard Parkes Bonington *Rouen* English 1825 (17.9 x 23.5cm)

Bonington (1802-28) died of consumption a few days before his twenty-sixth birthday. The painter Lawrence wrote, '... I have never known, in my own time, the early death of talent so promising.' Within a working life of perhaps seven years Bonington's output was prodigious. When he was 15, he moved with his parents from their native Nottingham via Calais to Paris. He was a pupil at the École des Beaux-Arts and, it was said, talked 'ceaselessly' of Turner and read Shakespeare, French histories and the romances of Sir Walter Scott. He was passionately interested in landscape and went on sketching expeditions, 'A knapsack on his back over his long blouse, a flat cap on his head and a stick in his hand.'

Rouen is a late summer evening view looking north-east across the Seine towards the three towers of Rouen Cathedral. (The cathedral is shown with a central spire which collapsed in 1822.) The lively foreground, touched with strokes of strong colour, is poetically contrasted with the grey-blue-pink tones of the middle distance.

Bonington spent a month in the spring of 1826 sketching in Venice. *Venice: the Piazzetta* is one of many sparkling watercolours based on the sketches he made. The view shows the south face of the Treasury of San Marco with the Pilastri Acritani columns in the foreground. The column of San Marco is seen in the distance across the Piazzetta. Delicate washes of pink and blue give life to sepia shadows and the red and ochre of tiny short-hand figures.

Richard Parkes Bonington *Venice: the Piazzetta* English 1826 (17.4 x 22.2cm)

Richard Parkes Bonington *Sunset in the Pays de Caux* English 1828 (19.8 x 26.3cm)

The Pays de Caux is the chalk plateau north of the Seine in Normandy which ends in spectacular cliffs at the Channel coast. *Sunset in the Pays de Caux* is one of Bonington's last watercolours and his most lyrical. It shows an adventurous Turneresque technique in the blotting out of the sun, the dragged dry colour in the sky and the atmospheric effects of light. The foreground figures and the luminous shadows on the cliff face are like the last line of a poem.

Richard Parkes Bonington *A Lady Dressing her Hair* English 1827 (15.2 x 10.2cm)

The lady, who wears early 17th-century Franco-Flemish dress, may be compared with Keats' *The Eve of St Agnes* (1819), '...her vespers done, /Of all its wreathed pearls her hair she frees.' In 1825, Bonington began to produce historical genre† pictures, described by the painter, Delacroix, as 'like diamonds.' Keats wrote that Bonington worked 'To make old prose in modern rhyme more sweet/ ... An echo ... in the north wind sung.'

The great age of English watercolour painting began in the late 18th century. Turner's brilliant essays in the medium helped raise its status. They showed its possibilities in rendering light, atmosphere and the fleeting movement of nature and weather. In the 1820s, English landscape painters became fashionable amongst younger French painters, who admired their fresh, vivid landscapes based on nature rather than other pictures. Bonington, then aged 21, was described as 'an Englishman brought to Paris whither he had brought the faith.'

John Mallord William Turner *Woodcock Shooting on Otley Chevin* English 1813 (28 x 39.8cm)

It is an autumn day on Otley Chevin, a hill two miles south of Otley in West Yorkshire, and one can almost smell the damp earth and fallen leaves. Turner painted *Woodcock Shooting on Otley Chevin* for Sir William Pilkington, who is the sportsman bringing his gun to his shoulder to shoot the woodcock surprised by the beater below. The Yorkshire landscape was an inspiration for Turner. He first visited the area when he was 18 and stayed with Walter Fawkes – Pilkington's brother-in-law – at Farnley Hall near Otley almost every year for 15 years.

Alexandre-Gabriel Decamps *Une odalisque* French c.1830-2 (44.6 x 36.3cm)

Une odalisque depicts a concubine in an Eastern harem. She must spend her days within the walls of the harem waiting for the visits of her master. Despite her rich clothes and jewels, her wistful look at the bird she holds on her finger expresses her desire to be as free as the flying birds seen through the open window. The chained monkey is perhaps a symbol of her imprisonment.

Projects to conserve antique armour and furniture are exhibited alongside explanations of the manufacture of armour, the process of gilding on metal and the technique of Boulle marquetry. Do not miss the chance to try on a Tudor breastplate or an English Civil War helmet.

Metals were given the appearance of solid gold by a process of mercury-gilding. Furniture mounts, described as gilt-bronze, are usually made of brass which was cast and chased[†] before a paste of mercury mixed with gold (in leaf or powder form) was applied. The mount was then heated, driving off the mercury in the form of highly poisonous fumes and leaving behind the gold, chemically fixed to the metal surface. Steel armour was hammered into shape while red hot. It was lightly copper-plated, by immersing it in a solution of copper salts, before being mercury-gilded.

Commode (chest of drawers), French 1735-40, detail
(in the West Gallery)

Maximilian I visiting his Court Armourer in his Workshop,
from *Der Weisskunig, c.*1512-16 (The British Museum, London)

French 18th-century furniture is made from a carcass of relatively cheap wood, such as pine or oak, with an eye-catching veneer, approximately 0.2cm thick, glued to the surface. Marquetry is a patterned veneer made up of different coloured woods or other materials such as metal, horn or mother-of-pearl. Boulle marquetry, named after the French cabinet maker, André-Charles Boulle (1642-1732), is usually made from turtleshell and brass. Flat layers of turtleshell and brass are sandwiched together and the design cut out with a special saw by a craftsman seated at a 'donkey' (a stool with a foot-operated vice).

Attributed to André-Charles Boulle, Toilet mirror
French 1713, detail (in the East Drawing Room)

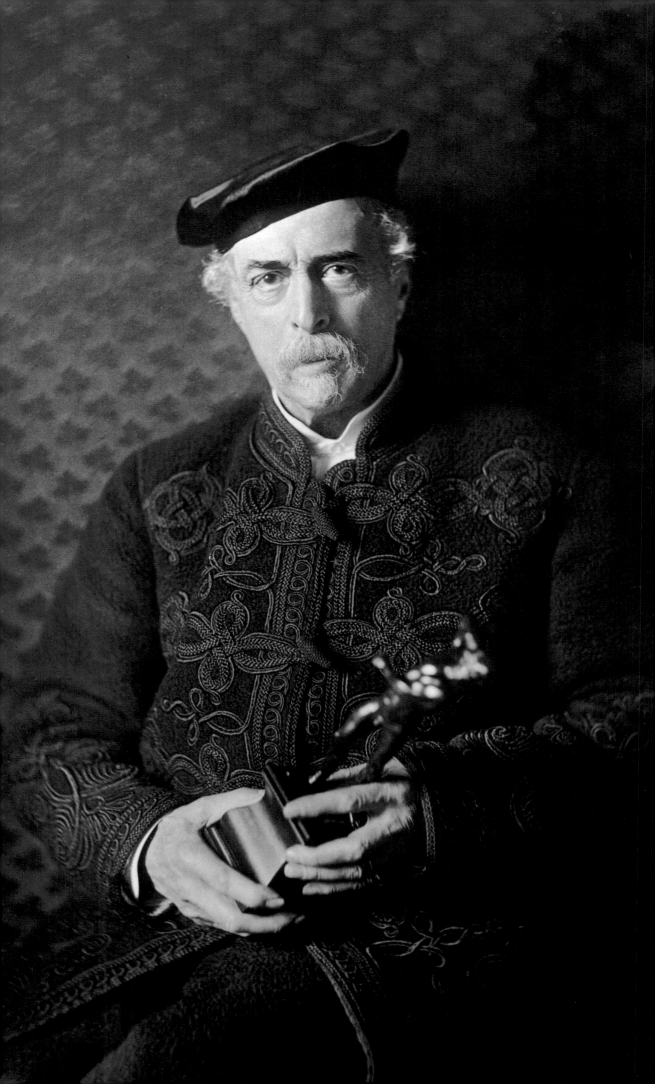

The Reserve Collection enables you to complete your tour of the entire Wallace Collection. Nothing is hidden from you in dark store rooms; you can see both inspired purchases and infrequent mistakes. Explore the vaults and discover drawers revealing Beauvais tapestry chair covers and Indo-Persian swords. One vault is devoted to the sticky subject of fakes and forgeries. Another will dazzle you with gold, silver and jewels.

Lady Wallace bequeathed the contents of the ground and first floors of Hertford House to the British nation and everything else to her late husband's secretary, John Murray Scott. Murray Scott's share, probably as rich in 18th-century French furniture as the present Wallace Collection, is now scattered all over the world. By the terms of the will, nothing was to be added to the Wallace Collection, and nothing taken away. The Wallace Collection is thus privileged in being able to preserve the tastes of one family, which altered over the generations, and to safeguard them against today's tastes, which will surely change as yesterday's did.

In the Wallaces' day, the vaults functioned as coal cellars, a vegetable larder and an ice vault.

Firescreen, French c.1760-70 (frame c.1845)
(tapestry: 86.5 x 66.2cm)

The firescreen is one of a pair. The tapestry, made in Lille, shows a peasant scene in the manner of the 17th-century Flemish painter, David Teniers the Younger. Outside an inn, a couple dance a jig to the accompaniment of a violin while another peasant raises his glass in salute. The inn sign is a crescent moon.

Sir Richard Wallace aged 70, 1888

	1720	1730	1740	1750	1760

**Francis Seymour-Conway
1719-94
1st Marquess of Hertford**

1719		1738	1741	1750	1762
Born		Grand Tour of France and Italy	Marries 15 year old Lady Isabella Fitzroy	Earl of Hertford	Ambassador to France
				1750s Bought 17th-century Dutch paintings in London salerooms	**1765** Lord Lieutenant of Ireland
			1743 1st son, Francis, is born		**1766** Lord Chamberlain, Royal Household

**Francis Ingram Seymour-Conway
1743-1822
2nd Marquess of Hertford**

1743	1750	1765
Born	Viscount Beauchamp	Chief Secretary to father
	1754-9 Attends Eton College	**1766** House of Commons
		1768 Marries Alice Elizabeth

Kings of Great Britain	Kings and Rulers of France
George I (1714-27)	Louis XV (1715-74)
George II (1727-60)	Régence (1715-23)
George III (1760-1820)	Louis XVI (1774-92)
Regency (1811-20)	Napoleon I (1804-15)

**Francis Charles Seymour-Conway
1777-1842
3rd Marquess of Hertford**

The Marquess of Hertford's eldest son is called the Earl of Yarmouth. His eldest grandson is called Viscount Beauchamp. When the Marquess dies, his son and grandson move up a rank.

1720	1734	1741	1751	1762
John Law's financial system crashes in Paris (May); South Sea bubble bursts in London (Sep)	J.S. Bach's *Christmas Oratorio*, Leipzig	Handel's *The Messiah*	Diderot's *La Encyclopédie*	Rousseau's *Social Contract*
		1745 Madame de Pompadour becomes Louis XV's mistress	**1752** Boucher's *The Setting of the Sun*	
1726 Swift's *Gulliver's Travels*	**1739** Louis XV's commode delivered to Versailles		**1759** Voltaire's *Candide*	

Fragonard *The Swing* 1767

1770	1780	1790	1800	1810	1814

Row 1

1770	1780	1790	1800	1810	1814
	1780s Ragley Hall, country seat, altered by James Wyatt **1782** Wife, Lady Hertford, dies **1785** Painted by Reynolds	**1793** Marquess of Hertford **1794** Dies			

Row 2

1770	1780	1790	1800	1810	1814
1772 1st wife dies **1774** Lord of the Treasury in Lord North's administration **1776** Marries Isabella-Anne Ingram-Shepherd	Isabella, Lady Beauchamp, aged 21	**1793** Earl of Yarmouth **1793** Special Emissary to forces opposing Revolutionary France **1794** 2nd Marquess	**1804** Master of the Horse, Royal Household **1807** Prince Regent falls in love with his wife, Isabella, 2nd Marchioness	**1812** Lord Chamberlain, Royal Household **1814** Ball at Hertford House to celebrate Napoleon's defeat	

Row 3

1770	1780	1790	1800	1810	1814
1777 Born	Francis Charles, aged 4	**1793** Viscount Beauchamp **1794** Earl of Yarmouth **1798** Marries Maria Fagnani (Mie-Mie) **1798** Tory MP	**1802** Visits Paris with Mie-Mie, who stays behind **1803** Returns to France but interned as an enemy alien **1805** Released	**1811** Prince Regent presents him with the Prince's portrait by Hoppner **1812** Appointed Vice-Chamberlain by the Prince Regent	

Row 4

1770	1780	1790	1800	1810	1814
		Richard Seymour-Conway 1800-70 4th Marquess of Hertford	**1800** Born Viscount Beauchamp **1802** Taken to Paris **1805** Half-brother, Lord Henry Seymour, born	**1800-** Lives in Paris with mother	

Row 5

1770	1780	1790	1800	1810	1814
1770 Lord North is British Prime Minister **1774** Marie-Antoinette is given le Petit Trianon **4 Jul 1776** American Declaration of Independence	**1 May 1786** Mozart's *The Marriage of Figaro* **14 Jul 1789** Storming of the Bastille **1789** George Washington is President of the USA	**1793** French Revolution: the Terror; France declares war on Britain, Holland and Spain **1795** The Directory governs France	**25 Mar 1802** Treaty of Amiens: Britain, Spain, Holland and France **1803** Peace fails **1805** Battle of Trafalgar	**1810** *De l'Allemagne* by Madame de Staël **1813** *Pride and Prejudice* by Jane Austen **11 Apr 1814** Napoleon defeated at Leipzig; exiled to Elba	

	1815	**1820**	**1830**	**1840**
	1815 Napoleon escapes from Elba (1 Mar); Battle of Waterloo (18 June) **1819** *Ivanhoe* by Sir Walter Scott	**23 Sep 1828** Bonington dies from consumption aged 25	**13 Jul 1830** July Revolution in Paris  Scheffer *Francesca da Rimini* 1835	**1848** Thackeray's *Vanity Fair*; Marx and Engel's *Communist Manifesto* **1848** Revolution in Paris: French Republic and Napoleon (later III) elected President

Francis Ingram
Seymour-Conway
1743-1822
2nd Marquess
of Hertford

1818
Presented with Gainsborough's *Mrs Robinson* by the Prince Regent

1820
Isabella, 2nd Marchioness, is replaced in George IV's affections

1822
Dies; dowager 2nd Marchioness continues to live at Hertford House

1834
Dowager 2nd Marchioness dies

Francis Charles
Seymour-Conway
1777-1842
3rd Marquess
of Hertford

1815
Purchases *Perseus and Andromeda* by Titian

1822
3rd Marquess

1823
Painted by Lawrence

1829
Moves to Dorchester House, Park Lane from Seaamore Place

1832
St Dunstan's Villa, Regent's Park, completed

1836
Lets Hertford House to the French Embassy

1841
Returns from last visit to France and Italy

1842
Dies

Richard
Seymour-Conway
1800-70
4th Marquess
of Hertford

1816
Brought to England for his education

1818
Matriculates at Exeter College, Oxford; has affair with Mrs Agnes Jackson, aged 28

1822
Earl of Yarmouth

1829
Acquires apartment at no.2 rue Laffitte, Paris

1835
Purchases château de Bagatelle, Bois de Boulogne, Paris

1838
Returns to Paris from journey in Italy

1842
4th Marquess

1845
Visits Irish estates

1846
Mistress, Mme Oger, has daughter

1848
Moves to 13 Berkeley Square, London

Sir Richard Wallace
1818-90

1818
Born Richard Jackson

1819
Amélie-Julie-Charlotte Castelnau born

1824
Richard Wallace lives in Paris with grandmother, 3rd Marchioness, and uncle, Lord Henry Seymour

1840
Mistress, Mlle Castelnau, has son, Edmond Richard

April 1842
Baptised 'Richard Wallace'

1843
Secretary to 4th Marquess

1850	1860	1870	1880	1890	1900

1851
Great Exhibition,
London

Dec 1851
Napoleon's *coup d'etat*

1854
Crimean War begins

1857
Madame Bovary by
Flaubert

1861
American Civil War
begins

1868
Benjamin Disraeli is
Prime Minister of
Great Britain

1870
Paris besieged by
Prussians

1871
Uprising of Paris
Commune (18 Mar)

1872
Tolstoy's *War & Peace*

1878
First electric light

1895
Freud publishes work
on psychoanalysis

1897
Queen Victoria's
Diamond Jubilee

10 Oct 1899
Boer War begins

Kings of Great Britain	Kings and Rulers of France
George III (1760-1820)	Louis XVIII (1815-24)
Regency (1811-20)	Charles X (1824-30)
George IV(1820-30)	Louis-Philippe (1830-48)
William IV (1830-37)	The Second Republic (1848-52)
Victoria (1837-1901)	Napoleon III (1852-70)
	The Third Republic (1871-1940)

1856
Dowager 3rd
Marchioness dies in
Paris

Lady Wallace
1819-97

1850
Returns to Paris

1855
Judge at Napoleon
III's Exposition
Universelle

1857
Lends 44 paintings
to Manchester Art
Treasures Exhibition

1865
Buys Hals' *The
Laughing Cavalier*
(27 Mar); buys
Fragonard's *The
Swing* (1 Jun)

1865
Lends to Musée
Rétrospectif
Exhibition, Paris

24 Aug 1870
Dies at château de
Bagatelle

1850s
Frequents salon of
Mme Sabatier

Nov 1856
Debts paid off by
4th Marquess

Mar 1857
Forced to sell art
collection by 4th
Marquess

1860
Mme Sabatier becomes
his mistress

Door panel from Mme
Sabatier's hôtel

Winter 1870/1
Chairman of British
Charitable Fund

15 Feb 1871
Marries Mlle Castelnau

Aug 1871
Created baronet

1872
Moves to London

14 Mar 1887
Son, Edmond Richard,
dies

1888
Lends to Old Masters
Exhibition, Royal
Academy

20 Jul 1890
Dies at château de
Bagatelle

16 Feb 1897
Lady Wallace dies

22 Jun 1900
The Wallace
Collection opens

ancien régime Political structure of pre-revolutionary France.

arabesque Rhythmic surface decoration based on patterns of scrolling and interlacing foliage and tendrils; Islamic in origin and adopted by Europeans during the Renaissance.

Arcadian Arcadia is the pastoral paradise of ancient Greek mythology.

blunderbuss Long-gun with widely flared muzzle intended to spread the shot (modern tests prove it does not).

chasing Finishing the surface of cast metal by removing blemishes and refining detail with a chasing tool.

chinoiserie Western evocations of Chinese art.

cornelian Semi-transparent quartz of deep dull red, pink or reddish white colour.

Cosimo de' Medici Grand Duke of Tuscany (1569-74). More powerful than any previous Medici ruler; a great patron of the arts, he created a court whose splendour rivalled the greatest courts of Europe.

dendrochronology Method of dating wooden panels.

Diderot (1713-84) French man of letters; edited *La Encyclopédie* 1751.

earthenware Made of secondary clays; impurities necessitate firing at low temperature so that after firing the clay is porous.

ebony Very fine-grained jet black tropical hardwood, sometimes streaked with yellow or brown.

falchion Short sword with a broad, single-edged blade and a double-edged point.

genre Category of painting best defined in the negative: not history, religious, portrait, landscape or still-life painting, i.e. scenes with figures and without a narrative from classical mythology or history.

gilt-brass or bronze Brass or bronze with a fine layer of gold applied to the surface – see Back State Room and Conservation Gallery.

gouache Opaque water-based paint made from gum arabic and a chalk-like filler.

grotesque Fanciful decoration – 'composition for delight's sake of men, beasts, birds, fishes, flowers …'; derives from renaissance discoveries of ancient Roman decorations in subterranean ruins known as 'grotte', hence 'grotesque'.

Japanese or Chinese lacquer Sap of the *rhus vernicifera* tree which becomes plastic on exposure to air – see Small Drawing Room.

jasper Variety of quartz, usually red, yellow or brown.

kris Characteristically-styled dagger of the Malay Archipelago.

lacquer Various kinds of resinous varnish.

Leda In ancient Greek mythology, Leda was loved by Jupiter, king of the gods, who came to her by the river in the form of a swan. He lay with her and she laid one or two eggs.

mercury gilding Method of gilding metal – see Conservation Gallery.

Ovid's *Metamorphoses* Ancient Roman poem telling tales of love and the magical transformation of forms.

pendant paintings A pair of paintings.

piqué Tortoise-shell or ivory inlaid with small studs and strips of gold or silver.

Psyche In Ovid's *Metamorphoses*, Cupid falls in love with the beautiful maiden Psyche and has her brought to his palace where he visits her only after dark, forbidding her to set eyes on him.

rapier Sword with a long narrow blade and a point, for thrusting rather than cutting.

Saint-Simon, duc de (1675-1755) French writer and courtier famous for his colourful and revealing memoirs of the closing years of Louis XIV's reign and the Régence.

Salon The French Royal Academy of Painting and Sculpture held annual or biennial salons at which academy members' work was exhibited.

satinwood Light-coloured hard wood with a rich silky lustre, from the *chloroxylon swietenia* tree found in India and Ceylon.

Sèvres porcelain Soft-paste and hard-paste (after 1768) porcelain produced by the Sèvres factory in France – see Back State Room.

shamshir Indo-Persian sword with a curved blade used for slashing cuts (also called 'scimitar').

silver-gilt Silver with a fine layer of gold applied to the surface.

sword or dagger

term Pedestal, tapering towards the base, with bust of a human, animal or mythical figure.

triptych Picture consisting of three parts, usually a focal central element flanked by two wings.

tulipwood Tropical hardwood from the *dalbergia* trèe; light coloured with a pronounced red grain resembling striped tulips.

tulwar Form of shamshir or scimitar with a characteristic style of hilt, usually Indian.

vanitas Moral warning that the acquisition of earthly treasures is mere vanity because the only certainty is death and eternal after-life, in either heaven or hell. Easily recognisable symbols ensure the message is not overlooked: candles are snuffed out like human life, hour glasses and watches remind us of the passing of time, skulls need no explanation.

vellum Fine calf-skin parchment.

vernis, French 18th-century French imitation of oriental lacquer on wood; applied in numerous coats; lustrous with a very fine texture and a wide range of colours; perfected by the Martin brothers.

Villa d'Este, Tivoli Elaborate villa constructed by Ippolito II d'Este of Ferrara in Tivoli, Italy, around 1550; known for its spectacular gardens.

Voltaire (1694-1778) French writer whose views epitomised the age of Enlightenment.

Wedgwood jasper-ware Fine-grained, slightly translucent stoneware perfected by the English potter, Josiah Wedgwood (1730-95); may be pure white or stained to a colour, e.g. the famous Wedgwood blue.